ON MISSION

TOGETHER

By
Richard Noble

FALLS CITY PRESS
Beaver Falls, Pennsylvania
www.fallscitypress.com

ON MISSION TOGETHER
Integrating Missions into the Local Church

© 2019 Falls City Press

2108 Seventh Avenue
Beaver Falls, PA 15010
www.fallscitypress.com

Cover Design by Rafetto Creative
www.rafettocreative.com

Publisher's Cataloging-in-Publication Data

Noble, Richard, 1967—

          p. cm.
    Includes bibliographical references.
    ISBN: (paper) 978-0-9864051-3-6

    1. Education and training of missionaries   I. Title.
BV2091.N67 2019

On Mission Together is a thorough manual for missions in the local church. It is rooted in the real church life and the extensive road experience that author Rich Noble has under his belt. It should prove exceptionally helpful for churches where intentional missions efforts are not staff matters but steered by committees of laypersons.

Tim Crouch, Vice President, Alliance Missions

With God's hand in the global migration of people, sharing the Gospel with the nations is not just work abroad, but it is also increasingly work at home. How can Christians be faithful and strategic in our mission? In this book, Rich offers us a thoroughly biblical and practical guide to participating in the Great Commission, whoever and wherever we are.

Liz Dong, Co-founder of Voices of Christian Dreamers

Rich's long—very long—involvement both in studying missions, as well as practicing them abroad and on the home front, provide one confidence that he has considered both the divine intent as well as human dimensions of the field. I have always found his grasp of all that is out there quite impressive, and his ability to bridge between what is denominationally and parachurch-based, quite impressive. His heart is with human souls, and that is where it should be when one aims to welcome believers to the activity of following Jesus by reaching outside of one's familiar zone and into the beyond.

Jonathan M. Watt, Chair of Bible, Christian Ministries, and Philosophy, Geneva College

Richard Noble has written an excellent overview on what church leaders should consider in global missions. This is an excellent primer for missions team members, missions pastors, or any church leader who seeks to understand the issues in local church missions.

Ted Esler, President, Missio Nexus

Contents

In honor of my dad and in memory of my mom—with much love and gratitude for the legacy you leave.

For my wife and children, with more love than words can express.

For all the local churches of the Western PA District of The Christian & Missionary Alliance as they seek to serve the Lord and follow His lead as participants in His mission, and especially for the saints at Washington Union Alliance Church in New Castle, Pennsylvania, with whom I had the privilege to serve in mission together for ten years as their pastor.

FOREWORD

Writing this foreword, let me begin with a few pertinent citations from the famous *Lausanne Covenant*.

> *Yet we who share the same biblical faith should be closely united in fellowship, work, and witness. We confess that our testimony has sometimes been marred by sinful individualism and needless duplication. We pledge ourselves to seek a deeper unity in truth, worship, holiness, and mission. We urge the development of regional and functional cooperation for the furtherance of the Church's mission, for strategic planning, for mutual encouragement, and for the sharing of resources and experience.*

(Article 7: Cooperation in Evangelism)

> *All churches should therefore be asking God and themselves what they should be doing both to reach their own area and to send missionaries to other parts of the world. A reevaluation of our missionary responsibility*

and role should be continuous. Thus, a growing partnership of churches will develop, and the universal character of Christ's Church will be more clearly exhibited.

(Article 8: Churches in Evangelistic Partnership)

More than 2,700 million people, which is more than two-thirds of all humanity, have yet to be evangelized. We are ashamed that so many have been neglected; it is a standing rebuke to us and to the whole Church. There is now, however, in many parts of the world an unprecedented receptivity to the Lord Jesus Christ. We are convinced that this is the time for churches and parachurch agencies to pray earnestly for the salvation of the unreached and to launch new efforts to achieve world evangelization. [...] The goal should be, by all available means and at the earliest possible time, that every person will have the opportunity to hear, understand, and receive the good news. We cannot hope to attain this goal without sacrifice.

(Article 9: The Urgency of the Evangelistic Task)

Rev. Dr. Richard A. Noble's book is written in, what Billy Graham called, "the spirit of Lausanne." The best and most succinct expression of that "spirit" is the *Lausanne Covenant,* a 1974 Evangelical Manifesto promoting active and cooperative worldwide Christian evangelization.

The *Lausanne Covenant,* one of the most influential documents in modern evangelicalism, was written under the editorial direction of John Stott, a globally renown pastor, evangelist and theologian, a man with a formidable intellect and ability to write with clarity and focus.

At the solemn conclusion of The First International Congress on World Evangelization in Lausanne, Switzerland, it was adopted with acclamation by more than 2,300 evangelical leaders from around the world. The first signatories of the Covenant were Rev. Billy Graham and the Australian Anglican Bishop Jack Dain. Many of us followed with a sense of deep commitment to the most holy and most urgent task of making the saving name of Jesus known among the nations. The *Lausanne Covenant* very quickly became a landmark basis for cooperative evangelism as the clearest articulation of the holistic Gospel. My personal participation as a 28 years old principal of a two-years young theological college (in the socialist country of Yugoslavia) changed my life. It was at Lausanne '74 that I learned that theology must serve the Kingdom of God and the church of Jesus Christ or else it is in danger of becoming a selfish academic enterprise. The Lausanne Congress and its Covenant impressed upon me the need for a holistic Gospel and the marriage of mission and theology.

I have learned at Lausanne that all theology must be missiologically focused and that all missions must be theologically (biblically!) grounded. I took the vision back to the young College in (former) Yugoslavia and shared it with my colleagues and students who caught the passion for world evangelization and church planting among the lost ethnic groups and cities all across the Balkans. The results were truly amazing, and its fruit is evident up to this day in all seven new countries that resulted from the break-up of now former Yugoslavia.

Reading the manuscript of this important book, I have reached the conclusion that Rich Noble thinks, writes, and acts in the "spirit of Lausanne." As if he were there personally and heard Ralph Winter remind us that there are still some 12,000 unevangelized people groups (*ethne*) who have never been reached with the Gospel of Jesus Christ.

Rich knows how to think biblically and holistically about world missions. I have observed his growth in vision, knowledge, and strategic engagement in his studies at

Gordon-Conwell Theological Seminary and in field explo-
rations, culminating with a well-written and practically relevant doctoral thesis-project *Recruiting a New Generation
of Missionaries: Doing Missions with Older Millennials in the
Christian and Missionary Alliance* (2004).

Rich's zeal for obeying Christ's Great Commission (Matthew 28 and parallel passages in other Gospels) burns brightly
and is accompanied by a prayerful attitude of expectancy for
God to bring to fruition the word of life as it is sown in the
harvest fields around the world.

Biblical insight, personal experience, and a vision
plus burden to reach people, yes, every person, with the
life-transforming message of the Gospel and to plant and
multiply Bible believing churches among the nations of the
world is part of Noble's vision about how to extend God's
Kingdom among the confused, lost, and disoriented king-
doms of this world.

In this almost comprehensive, well-organized, and very
helpful Manual for Missions, Richard Noble shares his heart
and mind with all who want to obey the Great Commission
of Christ. He himself has a proven record of performance
in missions as he practices and teaches it at Geneva College
and elsewhere around the world, including post-communist
Eastern Europe.

I recommend *On Mission Together* to every pastor and
elder in all local congregations and youth and adult Sunday
School classes for careful study and obedient application. If
we are to obey Jesus, we must continue and intensify the mobilization of the whole church to take the whole Gospel to the
whole world!

Peter Kuzmic, ThD
Professor of World Missions and European Studies
Gordon-Conwell Theological Seminary

ACKNOWLEDGMENTS

In the process of writing this book, it has occurred to me repeatedly just how many people have helped in the process. To all of you who have influenced my life regarding missions, I thank you for helping to form me along the way.

I especially thank the following people: my parents, Bob and Linda Noble, who instilled and modeled missions involvement for me and anyone else paying attention. All the pastors, youth pastors and leaders, Sunday school teachers, and other leaders at Westmont United Methodist Church in Johnstown, Pennsylvania, and Dorseyville Alliance Church in Pittsburgh, who invested in me as a child and teenager—teaching me the scriptures while nurturing a desire to see the peoples of this world reached with the gospel of Christ. Bob Bland, Gayle "Widder" Will, and the ministry of Teen Missions, International, who consistently fanned the flames of missions in my life. Brad Frey, Jack White, and the late Willard McMillan—professors of mine at Geneva College.

And Peter Kuzmic, Timothy Tennent, and the late J. Christy Wilson, Jr.—professors of mine at Gordon-Conwell Theological Seminary.

In terms of the book itself, special thanks to my editor and publisher, Keith Martel at Falls City Press, along with other editors and readers included in the process. Thank you also to those who served as beta readers, providing helpful conceptual input—Jerry Breedlove, Kylie Gibbons, Glenn Hanna and ACAC missions leaders, Jim Kendall, Susie Layton, Olivia Moore, Dean Smith, Sean Undercoffler, and students from the Geneva College Pittsburgh Campus as well as the Pennsylvania Bible Institute. Thank you also to those whom I interviewed about how missions is done at their church— their names and stories are featured throughout the book.

PREFACE

For as long as I can remember, my family has supported missions. I have always been interested in other cultures and the work of missionaries. As a child, I was intrigued by the mystique that accompanied the stories that I heard or read. I even started to collect money from other countries when I was nine. Even then, I loved anything that was international.

When I was twelve, I went on my first short-term missions trip with Teen Missions International (TMI) as part of a team that visited national parks throughout the southwest region of the United States to do evangelistic ministry for most of that summer. One of the great things about the Teen Missions experience happens right away with the two-week preparation process that happens at the Lord's Boot Camp in Merritt Island, Florida.

Throughout this training, the TMI staff is very intentional to create opportunities for exposure to missions and inviting participants to prayerfully consider their role in sharing the gospel with people from all nations. Along the way, one is pestered regularly by various insects. The most annoying of these bugs is not the mosquito or the gnat, as one might think. The most "irritating" bug is the missions bug because it just won't leave you alone. In a good way. It was there, at the Lord's Boot Camp and during my first experience with Teen Missions, that I was initially bit by this bug in a significant way–and I have never recovered.

A few years later I went with Teen Missions on two more trips: first to Germany between my junior and senior year in high school, then to Finland and Russia as one of the team leaders when I was in college. Needless to say, Teen Missions has played a significant part in influencing me and nurturing my enthusiasm for missions as it is there that I was first exposed to serving in missions in a direct and personal way. I have been blessed to have had such opportunities–and I am grateful for their ministry.

Over the years since, I have been on many other trips to various places all over the world with teams of people from college, seminary, and churches where I have served on pastoral staff. I have also been part of the staff of Envision, the short-term missions arm of The Christian & Missionary Alliance (then known as Alliance Youth Mission), and have been a denominational missions mobilizer with The Alliance in some capacity since 2001.

If you are reading this, it means you are also likely interested in missions and have the same desire to see God's people actively participating in His work around the world. That is why I am compelled to write this book—because I am obsessed with trying to motivate people to be a part of what God is doing throughout this world. You see, I am a missions mobilizer—a missions enthusiast who is deeply committed to seeing people engage in God's mission together.

As you read, you will find some basic principles that you can use to rally the people in your congregation around God's mission, specifically as it relates to God's work cross-culturally. This work all began in the early 2000s when I was completing my doctoral studies, which culminated in a dissertation that focused on recruiting the next generation of missionaries. Soon after completing that project, I realized that the same things that were true for engaging Millennials in missions were generally true for people of all ages, and I began to lead workshops and teach classes about these things.

Then, in 2009, I was invited to be part of a missions education group in The Christian & Missionary Alliance known as the Great Commission Education Creative Team, which involved co-writing a resource manual for The Alliance in 2013 called "On Mission." This book's roots grow from the soil of both my dissertation and "On Mission." It has been updated, revised, and expanded to reach a broader group of people like yourself, people who are excited about missions, people who desire to see their church be more actively engaged in the work of missions around the world.

The book begins with a brief introduction to the mission of God and the idea of partnering with God in this mission all the time, understanding that missions is not just a particular ministry program of the local church but rather a priority and a lifestyle for every follower of Jesus Christ. The next chapter continues with a biblical-theological overview of missions in the Bible so that we have a proper grasp of what it is that God desires of us in this regard. The second part of the book gets more practical by sharing principles gained over years of experience and practice, and a lot of listening, observing, and gleaning best practices from other churches and practitioners. Each chapter discusses a principle and ends with brief stories that showcase local churches that excel in putting that principle to work.

While the order of the chapters is intentional and, in some ways, builds off of one another, they can be read in whatever order you prefer—which may depend on the area you are most interested in. I have written with all church sizes and ethnic backgrounds in mind—and I believe that each of these principles can easily be applied to virtually any context in more specific ways, depending on the situation. If you're from a small church, please know that you can do missions just as exceptionally as the larger churches do it; if you're from a big church, we who are from the small churches know that you face many of the same challenges that we do when it comes to such things as educating people about missions, getting people to pray for missions regularly, and raising money for the work of missions.

Before you start reading, let me note just a few more things. First, much has been written elsewhere that defines, compares, and contrasts missions, mission, the missio Dei, and what it means to be missional. While these things are briefly defined in Part One, they are not extensively addressed. I did this because I do not want to detract from the bigger focus of the book, so I refer you to other more comprehensive works that develop this further. Second, I believe that we are all engaged in one mission that is expressed locally, regionally, and globally; the focus of this book is on the global component of our mission. Finally, the cover art for this book reflects a variation of the Agnus Dei in mosaic form—a powerful way of articulating the reign of King Jesus, the mission that He has sent us on, and the idea of many different parts contributing to the whole.

May the Lord richly bless you with insight as you explore the global component of engaging in mission together as the Church of Jesus Christ!

CHAPTER 1

IN PARTNERSHIP WITH GOD

"It is not so much the case that God has a mission for his church in the world but that God has a church for his mission in the world. Mission was not made for the church; the church was made for mission—God's mission."[1]

- Christopher J.H. Wright -

"The Church is a marvelous, mysterious creation of God that takes concrete shape in the lives of the disciples of Jesus as they gather in local congregations and seek to contextualize the gospel in their time and place... [A]s local congregations are built up to reach out in mission to the world, they will become in fact what they already are by faith: God's missionary people."[2]

- Charles Van Engen -

When I was in college, I finally watched a movie that some consider a classic: *The Blues Brothers*. In this film, the viewer is caught up in the adventures of two blood brothers who re-unite their band for a fundraising concert to try to save the financially troubled Catholic home and boarding school where they were raised. Part of what drives them to do this is their belief that they are on a "mission from God," simple belief that keeps them focused and moving forward to accomplish their goal. Over the years, I've heard many sermons and read more than a few books and articles that make the same connection that I have made: like the Blues Brothers, we who follow Jesus are on a mission from God. More specifically, we are partners in God's mission.

At first, this seems like a rather arrogant statement. However, once time is taken to soak in the statement and reflect on it from the teachings of scripture, it becomes clear that it is true. We are on a mission from God—and it is *His* mission. In fact, everything begins and ends with God, including missions. The obvious question now arises: What do I mean by this?

The Missio Dei. The proper place to begin this discussion is by looking at the *missio Dei*—the mission of God. What does this mean? What is God's mission? One way to answer this is by looking at God's story—and our story—as recorded in the Bible, which provides a framework for our understanding of who God is and what He is all about. The brief framework of this grand story, as briefly described below, is: Creation, Fall, Redemption, and Restoration.

Creation. The grand story begins with God, His glory, His creation, and His plan for creation. The scriptures tell us that God alone, in the persons of the Trinity, created out-of-nothing the entire universe and all that we know and experience by the power of His word as an act of His will. This activity was an actual event that marked the beginning of history and was declared "good" by God; it was perfect. The climax of this created work was humankind. We are each created in the image of God and are endowed with ethical and moral excellence. We are also each given the responsibility to care for God's creation as His stewards. All of this is only meaningful when we understand creation in relationship to God; the intent of creation is to turn our eyes to the Creator, who sovereignly reigns over and within that which He has created.[3]

Fall. The perfect world of pure fellowship with God and dominion over creation as God's stewards were destroyed after Adam and Eve sinned, breaking the relationship of trust that they had with God. In their pride, they sinned by revolting against God and His authority, doubting Him and rejecting Him while choosing to do things themselves. Their sin was a refusal to let God be God by trying to be God themselves.

This was not without devastating consequences. Our first parents were quickly evicted from perfect Eden into an imperfect world. The image of God in humans was now fractured, resulting in a distorted view of self, being afraid of God, broken relationships with other human beings, and separation from the world in which we live, resulting in our misuse/abuse of creation itself.

Because of their rebellion, and because Adam represented all of humanity, our ethical and moral excellence was permanently tainted and every human being who has ever lived has been born into sin, except Jesus Christ. There is no period of innocence for us, as we are each born with an innate desire of rebelling against God. We are corrupted and unable to truly know God, ultimately desiring to do only that which is wrong. We are full of guilt and have been sentenced to eternal death—endless separation from God and infinite, conscious torment in hell. We are all sinners, and we are all lost—this is the bad news.[4]

Redemption. The good news is that salvation, redemption from the Fall, is available to us because of God's amazing love and relentless pursuit of lost people of all races and ethnicities. Hope is not lost; salvation is available to us through Jesus Christ. His redemptive work on the cross and in the grave, announced by His resurrection and ascension, has delivered us from spiritual death and has rescued us from Satan, sin, and sin's results. Jesus died in our place, taking upon Himself God's anger and judgment so that God's honor and justice would be satisfied, and so that we could be reunited with God. While this has already happened, we are still required to repent of our sin and to fully trust God and His saving power for it to take effect. Truly, God rescues us by forgiving our sin and by changing our character—full rescue involves our change in lifestyle to reflect life lived under God's laws.[5]

Restoration. The grand story ends with Jesus Christ returning as King and Judge to establish the kingdom of God on earth, which He has already set in motion. On this day, Jesus will bring an end to history as we know it. Those who have placed their faith and trust in Jesus as Messiah and Savior will live forever in the presence of God in the new creation; creation will be restored/re-created and fully glorified. While various views of the end exist, we who follow Jesus all agree that, in the end, it's about Jesus and God's desire to have a people of all people groups love, serve, and worship Him.[6]

Understanding God and His desires in this way gives us insight into ourselves and the world we live in while shedding more light on our mission than what is found in a verse like John 3:16 or in the commands we are given in the Great Commission. Part of being on a mission from God includes telling His story to those who will listen.

Another way to look at the *missio Dei* is to simply understand that God is a missionary God; it's part of His nature.

Driven by His love for us, His purpose for the world is to call a people to be His own possession. He calls us to worship Him, to follow Jesus, and to live in His kingdom that He is establishing as we move toward the return of King Jesus and the arrival of the kingdom in its fullest and final expression. Of course, these eternal purposes of God have been and will be ultimately accomplished in the person and work of Jesus, who is the definitive expression of the *missio Dei*.[7]

As Jesus was sent by the Father and empowered with the Holy Spirit to accomplish redemption for us and establish God's kingdom on earth, so we, God's people, the Church, are sent by Jesus and empowered by the Spirit to participate in and extend God's mission as ambassadors of our King. Having experienced God's love ourselves, we live to love and worship God, to follow Jesus, and to make other lovers and worshipers of God and followers of Jesus. With the love of Christ in us, we are compelled to share in God's mission of love and mercy as the hands, feet, and voices of Jesus Himself who uses us to help build His Church around the world. We function this way not because God cannot do it Himself, but because He has chosen us to be His instruments in this world. The people of God are simply caught up in the mission of God; we are God's partners in mission, in our communities and around the world.

Partnering with God in Mission

What does it mean to partner with God in mission? It means coming alongside what God is already doing and allowing Him to use us in any capacity He desires, whether that's in our own community or on the other side of the world; it means living the mission. The Church, like God, is missionary by nature. As such, the Church has a missional makeup and is populated with missionary congregations.

It may be helpful to first understand what the Church is. We who follow Jesus are the Church, and together we are God's chosen covenant people, called to be distinct from the world. We exist together as the spiritual body of Christ in the world, both as the universal Church and as local congregations. Founded solely on Jesus Christ our head, who loved us, saved and purchased us with His blood, built us together as His people, and sanctified us, we put the kingdom of God on display in this world. We are a living organism which is created, populated, enriched with life, and empowered by the Holy Spirit. We are distinguished by our unity, our holiness, our universality, and our witness. We are characterized by the faithful and true proclamation and reception of God's Word, the correct administration of baptism and communion, and proper exercise of disciplinary action—all as commanded and instituted in scripture.[8]

In essence, we, the Church, are God's covenant community that has been called out of this world to worship and serve God and then sent back into the world as His representatives and agents of transformation. We are a people who bear witness to God's love and grace, lovingly serving the world and condemning its idolatry while proclaiming the presence of God's kingdom reign in Jesus Christ, which the Church expresses in an incomplete way. We are like sons and daughters who have inherited the family business and are absolutely committed to showing the world why our line of products is the best and are ultimately the only products that truly meet the needs of the consumer.

In short, as followers of Jesus, we each have a missionary vocation, in that we each participate in God's mission by declaring the good news of salvation while proclaiming the lordship of Jesus Christ to the world. That is not to say that all of us are missionaries. Missionaries, by definition, are those whom the Lord calls to minister in cross-cultural situations.[9] Rather, we are all expected to share this message within our local contexts, doing the work of evangelism. This one mission that we engage in is expressed at the local level (evangelism) and at the global level (missions). In fact, a congregation's local outreach efforts should feed into and encourage their global awareness and outreach, and vice versa. That being said, the core of being missional is Jesus Himself, who with His life and ministry gave us a model to learn and use. His pattern is simple: (1) worship God, (2) pray, (3) learn and obey God's teachings, (4) be together in fellowship with other Christians, and (5) spiritually reproduce by going and making disciples of Jesus and worshipers of the living God among all people groups. In partnership with God, the Church, made up of local congregations, is to be driven by this mission.

Missions as a Program vs. Missions as a Lifestyle

Reggie McNeal, a Missional Leadership Specialist for Leadership Network, describes the concept of being missional in this way, "The missional life shows up in every endeavor, because the church has been sent by God into the world to reflect his heart for the world. This is what it means to be on mission with God, *partnering with God*."[10]

What does this mean in terms of the *global* component of the missional life?

One very significant implication of global missional living is found in understanding that missions is not something to be added to a list of ministries within the local church as an afterthought. Missions is something that is central to the plan and purposes of God for humanity. As such, God's mission is our priority in *all* ministries of the local church, not just one ministry program of many. Missions, therefore, is a lifestyle.

Dr. Robert Fetherlin, former Vice President of International Ministries for The Christian & Missionary Alliance (C&MA), provides some insight here by identifying five tensions that help make this distinction between local church missions programs and missional living. The five tensions are as follows:

1. Spoke vs. Hub—The missions program is one of many spokes in the church's ministry, whereas missional living is the hub of the wheel; instead of being championed by just a few people, Christ's mission is embraced as the center of everything the church does.

2. Seven vs. 365—The church missions program may focus on a missions conference or missions fair that is slanted toward denominational concerns, while missional living injects missions (i.e., God's mission and our part in it) into the DNA of the church and how the church does ministry, with a focus on what God is doing throughout the whole world. Missions focus is not confined to a map of the world that fades into the background or into the announcements in the church bulletin; it is the engine the drives the church forward in the power of the Holy Spirit.

3. Few Sparks vs. Raging Fire—The missions program has pastors and leaders who feel obligated to participate in missions, sharing the missions sparks they have in their heart, as opposed to missional living where pastors and leaders passionately lead the church in expressing its global commitment, sharing the missions fire that burns in their heart; instead of having glowing embers of mission with occasional sparks flying, church leaders keep the flames of the missional fire dancing into the hearts of people and church ministry programs.

4. Handshake vs. Holding Hands—The church out-sources missions to missionaries with whom they have little personal contact, whereas missional living involves being strongly connected to those who have been sent, working together with them in partnership for the sake of the gospel of Christ and His kingdom; missionaries are seen as co-laborers with whom the congregation collaborates, rather than as people to whom the church sends money and offers prayers.

5. Praying from a Distance vs. Owning—The church missions program involves writing checks to and praying for missionaries from a distance, while missional living suggests that the people of the local church are directly and personally involved in the work; because everyone in the church has an important role to play in the work of missions, not just our bank accounts should be impacted.[11]

What does a year-round missions awareness look like, where living on mission is part of the DNA of the congregation? The following elements are present and will be explored in more detail in the second part of this book:

Missions Awareness, Ministry Events, and Education. Missions-minded churches have an enthusiastic commitment to missions where God's mission is seen as the priority and focus of church ministry. Missions is integrated into *all* the church's ministry programming, including children, youth, and adults. Here, the people are regularly informed about missions or are given missions-related updates in public worship services and are regularly informed about missions or are given missions-related updates in Sunday school classes and small groups; information about missions is included in worship service bulletins, as well. Many churches who champion missions often conduct an annual missions conference or other types of missions emphasis events throughout the year, many times hosting missionary speakers or international guests. People in such churches also know and understand what the Bible teaches about missions and understand what missions is.

Praying for Missions and Missionaries. Churches that are passionate about missions corporately pray for the work of missions and missionaries in worship services, Sunday school classes, and small groups. People are also regularly provided with up-to-date information and prayer requests from missionaries who are known and supported.

Giving to Missions. Missional churches give money to missions ministry, including organizations outside the denomination. Missions giving is strategic and specific, and people understand the vehicle for giving to missions and know where the money is going.

Sending and Caring for Missionaries. Missionaries who have been sent from the church or who call a local church "home" are prayed for and financially supported in churches that are committed to being on mission together. People also regularly communicate with these missionaries and take care of and minister to them when they are "home."

Missions Exposure and Ministry Experiences. In missions-oriented churches, there are opportunities for cross-cultural ministry in which people can get involved. Indeed, the church is directly engaged in the mission through short-term missions experiences and global ministry partnerships, and people are involved with cross-cultural ministry in the community by serving internationals who live there. Additionally, multicultural church ministry is taken into consideration.

Church Leadership and Missions. Churches that are driven by missions have pastors and other church leaders who are committed to and enthusiastic about missions, motivating and equipping people to be fully engaged. Typically, there is an organized and effective missions leadership team to help provide this kind of leadership to the congregation.

Identification of Future Missionaries. Churches that have missions in their DNA to identify, encourage, and equip potential/future missionaries as people (especially children and teenagers) are encouraged to consider that God may be calling them to "vocational ministry/missions." In such congregations, the people pray for missionaries to be raised up and sent out from within their community.

Conclusion

Many people and congregations desire to live the christian life missionally; they genuinely want to live the mission and be on mission together. However, they often do not have a level of faith, love, and courage to truly do that. As followers of Jesus, we should strive to live our lives as an act of humble worship before the Lord. This requires us to live a life of love and faith, of courageous risk-taking, and of sacrifice and service. It is true that living this way will often be messy, unscripted, and uncontrollable. But such a life is a life committed to living the mission. As such, we ought to be *missionary congregations*, not just inward-looking churches with missions programs. Missions, or missional living, should be integrated into every ministry program of the local church. We are, after all, partners with God in His work around the world; God's mission is our mission and we are God's missionary people.

Suggested Resources

David J. Bosch. *Transforming Mission: Paradigm Shifts in Theology of Mission.* Maryknoll, NY: Orbis Books, 1991. (Part Three)

Reggie McNeal. *Missional Renaissance: Changing the Scorecard for the Church.* San Francisco: Jossey-Bass, 2009.

John Stott and Christopher J.H. Wright. *Christian Mission in the Modern World,* updated and expanded ed. Downers Grove: IVP Books, 2015.

Charles Van Engen. *God's Missionary People: Rethinking the Purpose of the Local Church.* Grand Rapids: Baker Book House, 1991.

Christopher J.H. Wright. *The Mission of God's People: A Biblical Theology of the Church's Mission.* Grand Rapids: Zondervan, 2010.

Notes

[1] Christopher J.H. Wright, *The Mission of God: Unlocking the Bible's Grand Narrative* (Downers Grove: IVP Academic, 2006), 62.

[2] Charles Van Engen, *God's Missionary People* (Grand Rapids: Baker Book House, 1991), 17.

[3] See Genesis 1-2, Job 38:1-11, Psalms 8, 19:1-6, 33:6-9, 104:24-32, 136:1-9, Proverbs 8:22-31, Isaiah 40:21-31, John 1:1-18, Acts 17:24-25, and Colossians 1:15-20.

[4] See Genesis 6:5, Numbers 15:38-41, 1 Kings 8:46, Psalms 14:1-3, 51:1-6, 53:1-3, Isaiah 53:6, Jeremiah 17:9, Ezekiel 36:26, John 8:34, Romans 3:9ff, 5:12-14, 6:19-23, 8:18-21, Galatians 5:19-21, and 1 John 1:8.

[5] See Genesis 3:15, 6:9-8:22, 11:27-25:11, Exodus 12:1-30, Leviticus 4:1-5:13, 16:1-34, 25:1-55, Numbers 21:4-9, Deuteronomy 7:7-11, Psalms 22 & 51, Isaiah 52:13-53:12, Ezekiel 36:24-28, Jesus' death and resurrection accounts in the gospels, John 1:29, 3:1-21, Acts 2:22-36, 3:11ff, 4:8ff, Romans 3:21-26, 5:1-21, 1 Corinthians 15:1-11, Titus 3:3-8, and Hebrews 4:14-5:10 and 9:1-10:18.

[6] See Psalms 2:1-12, 22:25-31, 24:7-10, 96:13, 98:9, Isaiah 11:1-5, 63:1-3, 65:17-19, Matthew 3:7-12, 24:23-44, 25:31-46, Luke 16:19-31, John 5:22-29, Acts 1:6-11, Romans 8:18-25, 1 Corinthians 15:12-57, Ephesians 1:20-23, Philippians 2:9-11, 1 Thessalonians 4:13-18, Titus 2:11-14, 1 Peter 1:3-9, 2 Peter 3:13, and Revelation 1:4-8, 19:11-16, 21:1-22:6.

[7] Theologian Edmund Clowney said it this way: "Our fearful condition as lost sinners forms the dark horizon where God's grace brings the dawn of hope. In the Bible, salvation is God's mission to a lost world. It is God who seeks Adam and Eve in the garden; God who promises the Son of the woman who will crush the head of the serpent; God who warns Noah, and calls Abraham in Ur and Moses at the burning bush. The book of Judges, the narratives of the books of Kings and the words of the prophets all point to the golden text of the Old Testament: 'Salvation comes from the LORD' (Jon. 2:9).

God himself must come to bring his salvation. This is the *missio Dei*. God accomplishes his saving mission by sending his Son into the world. Jesus is the great Missionary, sent by the Father." (Edmund P. Clowney, *The Church* (Downers Grove: InterVarsity Press, 1995), 158-159.

[8]This understanding of the Church cannot—and must not—be separated from the mission of the Church; the two belong together.

[9]Missiologist Herbert Kane provides a classic definition of missionary: "In the traditional sense the term missionary has been reserved for those who have been called by God to a full-time ministry of the Word and prayer (Acts 6:4), and who have crossed geographical and/or cultural boundaries (Acts 22:21) to preach the gospel in those areas of the world where Jesus Christ is largely, if not entirely unknown (Romans 15:20). This definition, though by no means perfect, has the virtue of being Biblical." (Herbert Kane, *The Making of a Missionary*, 2nd ed. (Grand Rapids: Baker Book House, 1987), 14.) Missions leaders Denny Spitters and Matthew Ellison add that all "Christians are called to participate in the Great Commission – globally as well as locally, we would say. All are included in God's global mission. But not all Christians are called to be apostolic missionaries." (Denny Spitters and Matthew Ellison, *When Everything is Missions* (Orlando: BottomLine Media, 2017), 72.

[10]Reggie McNeal, *Missional Renaissance: Changing the Scorecard for the Church* (San Francisco: Jossey-Bass, 2009), 26.

[11]Robert Fetherlin, "The Mindset of the Missional Church" (talk given to C&MA missions mobilizers at a conference at Westgate Chapel in Toledo, OH on 25 March 2006).

CHAPTER 2

WHAT THE BIBLE
SAYS ABOUT MISSIONS

"Beginning with Genesis and ending with Revelation, book after book and scripture after scripture yields abundant evidence that God loves us and offers us hope that springs forth as an antidote to the poison called sin. In fact, in one way or another, every book of the Bible renders testimony of God's heart for the peoples of the world."[1]

- Leonidas A. Johnson -

"Without the Bible, world evangelization would not only be impossible but actually inconceivable. It is the Bible that lays upon us the responsibility to evangelize the world, gives us a gospel to proclaim, tells us how to proclaim it and promises us that it is God's power for salvation to every believer."[2]

- John R.W. Stott -

Let me begin this chapter with three brief and significant theological statements about the Bible (I can't help it, it's the preacher and Bible teacher in me). First, as followers of Jesus, we consider the Bible to be inerrant. It is without error of any kind and it is true in all that it affirms. Second, as followers of Jesus, we embrace the Bible as God's voice of authority in our lives. It is the defining point for all the Church's teaching, faith, and life; truly, God speaks to us through His Word. Third, we believe that God's word is sufficient for us. It contains all we need to understand what is required for salvation as it leads us to God's mercy and redemption and reveals all the guidelines we need regarding how to live a righteous life. I bring this up because I believe that being engaged in the missional lifestyle involves turning to God's inerrant, authoritative, sufficient word for instruction and insight. Indeed, knowing what the scriptures say on this matter will help us better know and understand the heart of God as it relates to missions.

Having such a biblical overview of missions will help build a stronger foundation for understanding the *missio Dei*, missions, and our role in God's global plan by anchoring us more fully to the story of God that we briefly discussed in Chapter One. Embedded within this story is the theme of God's faithful love for the people He created, who have rejected God and His love repeatedly. In spite of this, driven by this love, God redeemed His people, offers them relationship and eternal life in His kingdom, and calls them to a life of loving, serving, and worshiping Him. One lens to read this love story through is the lens of missions; after all, God is a global God who deeply loves all peoples of the earth.

Get ready—this chapter is going a little deeper than the others in terms of content. Don't skip this material. Resist the temptation to just scan over it. And as you read, also take the time to pore through the scriptures presented, allowing God's voice to speak refreshing words of love and purpose.

Missions in the Old Testament

When establishing a theology of missions, there is a temptation to ignore the Old Testament and proceed immediately to the New because that is where the teachings of the Lord Jesus are recorded. To overlook the Old Testament in terms of missions, though, is a mistake. Not only is the Old Testament a vital part of our scriptures, but we see in them that even a quick examination of Israel's historical writings, poetry, and prophecies reveals that God has always loved and been concerned for all peoples from all nations.[3] I encourage you not to ignore this footnote that you possibly read right past. Please take some time to look up the various Old Testament passages that are identified there to help give you a better glimpse into the heart of God.

As this chapter is intended to not provide an extensive study of missions in the Bible, but rather a general overview, Dr. Walter Kaiser's abridged approach of missions in the Old Testament[4] will be taken here. That is, a summary of missions in the Old Testament may be found in three key passages: Genesis 12:1-3, Exodus 19:4-6, and Psalm 67.

Genesis 12:1-3 records that God made a covenant with Abraham where He promised to: (1) bless him with many descendants, (2) bless his descendants by making them into a great nation, and (3) bless all the peoples of the earth through his descendants (see also Genesis 17:1-8, 18:18, 22:17-18, and 28:13-14). Why would God do this? The answer lies in verse 2: to share God's blessing with others.[5] This principle applies not just to Abraham. When the rest of his story is read, we find that his descendants become the nation of Israel—a people chosen by God to be *His* people. As the rest of Scripture is studied, we further discover that those who place their trust in Jesus for salvation are also children of God and spiritual descendants of Abraham. So, the principle exists for both Israel and the Church: we who are God's people are blessed in order to be a blessing to others by bearing witness to God's deeds of grace, mercy, and salvation to the peoples and nations of the world so that they, too, may be counted among the children of God. Pastor and theologian John Piper says it well, "What we may conclude from [this passage]…is that the blessing of Abraham, namely, the salvation achieved through Jesus Christ, the seed of Abraham, would reach to all ethnic people groups of the world."[6]

Exodus 19:4-6 provides tremendous insight into God's missionary heart, showing the covenant relationship that He had with Israel. In essence, this passage shows that if the people of Israel obeyed God and the stipulations of the covenant that He had established with them, then they would be:

(1) God's own possession among all the peoples of the earth,
(2) a kingdom of priests who would be faithful witnesses of God and His deeds,
(3) a holy nation that would be set apart from the nations to serve God.

As we see in the passage, this divine election of Israel brought with it an obligation to be a channel of God's blessing to the nations, rather than a privilege reserved only for God's elite (see also Deuteronomy 28:9-10). In other words, God's "blessing came to Israel as a means of reaching the nations."[7] As Walter Kaiser put it, the "whole purpose of God was to bless one people so that they might be the channel through which all the nations of the earth might receive a blessing. Israel was to be God's missionaries to the world, and therefore, so are all who believe in this same gospel."[8]

The book of Psalms records "more than 175 references of a universalistic note relating to the nations of the world. Many of them bring hope of salvation to the nations."[9] Psalm 67 is one such reference, reaffirming the promises made to Abraham in Genesis 12:1-3[10] and indicating God's desire to bless the nations of the earth. The psalm begins with a request for God to extend His grace upon Israel and to bless her. Why? So that His way and His salvation would be known among all the nations of the earth. To what end? So that all peoples would share in Israel's gladness as God's people, singing for joy and offering praises to God. The principle of being blessed by God to be a blessing to others is noted again at the end of the psalm (verse 7): God blesses His people so that all the people of the earth will fear (trust, obey, worship) the one true God. This psalm clearly expresses the missions dynamic that is present throughout the Old Testament—the hope "that God might be praised and that this doxology must be offered by all the peoples of the world."[11]

From the very beginning, we see that God has always loved peoples from all nations and ethnic backgrounds. Of course, this does not change as we begin reading the New Testament. If anything, we see that love intensified–and we see with even more clarity and fervency how we are to share that love with the rest of the world as we live as God's people.

The Great Commission

The Church's primary missions directive is found in the four gospels and in Acts—the Great Commission that was issued by the risen Jesus. Though given originally to Jesus' apostles, it is a commission for all who follow Jesus in all generations to obey until Jesus returns.

In Matthew's account (Matthew 28:16-20), authority is given by Jesus to the Church to evangelize, baptize, and teach. It is a general commission in which the main objective is to make lifelong disciples—not just converts—of Jesus Christ while planting churches on a global scale. This process involves evangelizing non-Christians, baptizing new believers into the community of faith, and teaching the doctrines and commands given to us by Jesus. This means helping people to live like Jesus in a way where all areas of life are committed to the lordship of Jesus and submitted to the reign, love, and justice of God. There is an emphasis here on crossing ethnic frontiers with the gospel of Jesus Christ. There is also a promise from Jesus included here, a promise that He will lead the way for His people and never leave the Church.

Mark (Mark 16:14-18)[12] keeps it simple yet comprehensive. It places an emphasis on preaching the events, affirmations, demands, and promises of the gospel across geographical frontiers and proclaiming to the whole world the arrival of God's kingdom in Jesus. Evangelism here involves proclaiming the gospel to persuade people to decide to follow Jesus, obey His teachings, and be part of the community of faith. It is the responsibility of those who receive this message to take further action by repenting.

Luke's version (Luke 24:44-49) is not so much a command as it is a promise that repentance and forgiveness will be preached in Christ's name to all the nations. For Luke, the emphasis is on the primary calling of the Christian to be a witness for Jesus Christ and His redemptive act of salvation. Evangelism here involves being empowered by God's Spirit to share in the *missio Dei* by going to the entire world to share the message of Christ's forgiveness and the repentance of sins. This is the only version of the commission that includes the specifics of the gospel message itself.

John (John 20:19-23) is also very simple and to the point. The Church, empowered by God's Spirit, is sent into the world by Jesus to bear witness to the things of God, just as Jesus Himself had been sent. This task originates in God's heart and its fulfillment depends on a relationship with Him. Also seen here is that the commission is centered on Jesus Christ, for He is the model of the Church's mission. His mission is the Church's mission. Indeed, the exalted Jesus actually continues His mission through the Church.

The book of Acts (Acts 1:6-8) reveals that the momentum for the Great Commission comes from the Holy Spirit, who enables the Church to take part in the *missio Dei.* The aim of the Church's mission here is to bear witness to the life, ministry, and atoning work of Jesus, while exhorting people to believe, repent, and receive salvation. Again, there is stress laid on crossing ethnic and geographical frontiers with this universal message. The book of Acts also thoroughly reveals what it looks like when the Church lives in obedience to the Great Commission as the story of the first-century Church unfolds (see Acts 8:25-40, 9:10-22, 10:24-11:26, 13:1-14:28, 15:36-18:23, and 18:23-21:6).

When all these passages are taken together, the directive from Jesus sounds like this, as pieced together from the New International Version:

> *Peace be with you! All authority in heaven and on earth has been given to Me [and] I am going to send you what My Father promised; receive the Holy Spirit. When the Holy Spirit comes on you, you will receive power, and you will be My witnesses in Jerusalem, and in all Judea and Samaria, and to the ends of the earth. This is what is written: The Messiah will suffer and rise from the dead on the third day, and repentance for the forgiveness of sins will be preached in His name to all nations, be-*

ginning at Jerusalem. You are witnesses of these things.
Therefore, go into all the world and preach the gospel to
all creation—and make disciples of all nations, baptizing
them in the name of the Father and of the Son and of the
Holy Spirit, and teaching them to obey everything I have
commanded you. Whoever believes and is baptized will
be saved, but whoever does not believe will be condemned.
And these signs will accompany those who believe: In My
name they will drive out demons; they will speak in new
tongues; they will pick up snakes with their hands; and
when they drink deadly poison, it will not hurt them at
all; they will place their hands on sick people, and they
will get well. If you forgive the sins of anyone, their sins
are forgiven; if you do not forgive them, they are not for-
given. As the Father has sent Me, I am sending you—and
surely, I am with you always, to the very end of the age.

Paul never really set out a clear command to the Church to
go to the ends of the earth bearing the message of the gospel
to all people as Jesus did. However, three passages in Romans
give insight into what Paul's thoughts were concerning the
Great Commission.

In Romans 1:1-6, Paul begins his letter to the Romans by
sharing his charge to invite people to obey God, even as he
himself is driven to obey God and to reach others with the
gospel. The goal of all his work was to call men and women
from all nations and people groups to a faith relationship
with the Lord Jesus. This is part of the model that Paul has
provided for the Church, an example that suggests that since
Jesus is Lord, then His people ought to share in His passion
to give the gospel to all people. Indeed, all Christians are presented with the same mission as Paul's: to participate in God's
mission to the world.

The second insightful passage is Romans 10:14-21 where Paul raises the issue of how people who believe the message of the gospel are able to call on the name of the Lord only after they hear someone preach the gospel to them—someone who first has to be sent. The key verse here, in terms of our directive, is verse 15, which states that preachers of the gospel need to be sent in order for their message to be heard. "Unless some people are commissioned for the task," John Stott wrote, "there will be no gospel preachers."[13] As John Calvin put it, the "gospel does not fall like rain from the clouds, but is brought by the hands of men wherever it is sent from above."[14] As the Church, we should be people who are driven, as Paul was, by the love of Jesus, empowered by God's Spirit, and sent throughout the world to bring the message of the gospel of hope and peace to all who will hear.

The third insight is gained from Romans 15:14-22 where Paul's final thoughts to the Romans provides an overview of his missionary career and reinforces that he is a world-Christian who, like Jesus, is driven to reach the lost by preaching the gospel throughout the world to those who have never heard.[15] Again, as the Church we are given the same responsibility that Paul was given, to take the love and message of Jesus Christ to all people around the world.[16]

As one looks at these passages, along with the book of Acts and other letters of Paul, one finds that he did not need to instruct people about the Great Commission with words because his life itself bore witness to the importance of the Great Commission lifestyle.

Like Paul, Peter did not give a clear command to evangelize and make disciples of all peoples. But, like, Paul, he did provide some insight into the Great Commission with one other significant instruction given to the Church in 1 Peter

2:4-10. In this passage Peter recalls Exodus 19:4-6 and teaches that the Church is: (1) God's chosen people who are a spiritual building of living stones that are being built on the foundational cornerstone of Jesus; (2) A royal priesthood: a "group of priests who belong to a king"[17]—who have full access to God through Jesus Christ, as well as a priestly duty to do ministry (in the Church and in the world); (3) A holy nation: holy, moral people who reflect God's holiness in the world; and, (4) A peculiar people who belong to God and who are separate from the world yet live in the world as God's ambassadors. As such, the Church exists to worship God by offering spiritual sacrifices of praise, thanksgiving, acts of charity, and mutual sharing; God redeemed His people to bring glory to His name. Furthermore, the Church exists to make other worshipers of God and disciples of Jesus Christ by proclaiming God's message of grace and mercy to the world. Peter's grasp of the Great Commission, then, is simply this: worship God above all else and go make disciples and worshipers of the living God among all people.

As alluded to earlier, this commission for Christians is Trinitarian in nature: God sent His Son, the Son sends the Church, and the Holy Spirit goes with it. The mission of the Church is inspired by God, centered on Jesus Christ, and directed by God's Spirit. Living in obedience to the final command of Jesus is not just a program that exists *within* local congregations, it is what the Church *is* and what the Church *does*. The Church ought to be driven by this mission, not from a sense of duty but from a sense of privilege. We serve not because we have to, but because we want to and because we get to.

Other Insights from the New Testament

The Great Commandment. The Great Commission is not complete without the Great Commandment that is recorded in Matthew 22:34-40/Mark 12:28-34 and in Luke 10:25-28. In the first instance, Matthew and Mark record that after an intense discussion with the Sadducees about the final resurrection, a Pharisee, who was an expert in Jewish law, approaches Jesus to test Him by asking what the greatest, most important command from God was. The answer was simple and agreeable to the law expert: love the one Lord God with the whole heart, soul, mind, and strength, and love your neighbor as yourself.

After the seventy returned from their evangelistic mission, Luke records another time when an expert in Jewish law approached Jesus with a different question to test Him, asking what must be done to inherit eternal life. This time Jesus put it back on the law expert, who rightly answered that it required loving God with all of one's heart, soul, strength, and mind as well as loving one's neighbor as oneself. Jesus further clarified what a neighbor was by telling the story of the "good Samaritan." Essentially, we who follow Jesus are expected to first love and serve God with total devotion and then love and serve other people; this is God's entire law in summary form. The principle is simple. Love God, love others. Good works (seen in loving others) stem from loving God first as God's love within produces a love for others. Jesus, of course, set the standard for this.

Salt and Light. This is an image of the Church's mission that is found in Matthew 5:13-16. To be salt and light in the world involves loving other people and setting a proper example of God's holiness for a sinful world. One of salt's main purposes is helping to stop meat from decaying and becoming rotten; it purifies and preserves the meat, while also adding flavor to it. This process works only by direct contact with the meat and though the salt will disappear within the meat, it cannot and will not lose its saltiness. While salt is a stable compound that resists almost anything, it can be contaminated when it is mixed with certain impurities. When this

happens, salt becomes useless and is not even good for a ma-
nure pile or compost heap.

The image given here is that we need to live in a way
that is distinct from the world, without being identical to
it as we follow Jesus. If the Church becomes too much like
the world, then she becomes useless. We therefore need to
be in direct contact with the world (as salt is with meat)
so that we may not only add flavor to it but also help stop
its decay. This means living lives with integrity, excellence,
purity, honesty, and fairness.

The primary function of light is to penetrate and illumi-
nate the darkness. The image here is that through our works
of love and faith, Christ is seen, and God is glorified in the
process. The world is a spiritually dark place (some places
darker than others), and the Church exists within an age of
darkness. Jesus said in John 8:12 that He was the "Light of
the world." As God's representatives, we are beacons of light
in this dark world. Jesus must shine through the Church—in
local congregations—in word and deed.

Salt and light very simply change the environments that
they come in contact with; just a little of each goes a long way
to do that. Being salty and bright is their very character, not
how they act. In the same way, salty and bright is what we are
to be as the Church; it's not just what we do, it is a reflection
of God's reign in our midst. True allegiance to Jesus alone is
reflected in everyday life in the home, in the school, in the
community, and in the workplace. God will bless these efforts
and salvation will be brought to others as God is glorified.
This kind of lifestyle was clearly seen in Jesus Himself, who is
the perfect example.

Be Ambassadors. In 2 Corinthians 5:16-21 Paul states that as
people who are newly created in Christ Jesus and reconciled to
God, we have a ministry of reconciliation in the world. Followers

of Jesus, it is said in verses 19-20, are expected to be God's spokespersons that bear to the world the message that God is reconciling the world to Himself in Jesus; God makes His appeal to the world through His people who are His ambassadors that make known the benefit of an invitation to being reconciled with God. As God's people in this world, then, we are God's voice in and to the world, acting and speaking for God with His authority[18] and direction. This also means that each local church exists as an embassy of God's kingdom within the community of which it is part—our church buildings partly exist as our headquarters where we live and minister as Christ-followers as we relate to the general public, just as embassies and consulates of the nations do throughout the world.

God and the Nations

Throughout the Bible, it is clear that God has a special concern for *all* nations and peoples of the earth to worship Him and experience His grace, forgiveness, and faithfulness within an open covenant relationship of trust in Him through Jesus Christ. As John Piper points out, the Old Testament alone is full of this hope for God to reach all peoples of the world, particularly in Psalms and Isaiah. Piper notes that this is seen in four ways: (1) exhortation: that God's glory would be declared and that God would be praised among the nations and by the nations; (2) promise: that nations will someday worship the true God; (3) prayers: that God would be praised among the nations; and (4) plans: to help make God's greatness known among the nations.[19]

The sentiment is equally clear in the New Testament, particularly with the teaching of Jesus. Not only did He give us

the task of worldwide evangelism and disciple-making, but
He also gave us a great hope and motivation to do so.

In Matthew 24:14 and Mark 13:10, a simple statement
made by Jesus about His return is recorded. Here, Jesus told
His disciples that He would not return until the job was done.
That is, Jesus told us that one of the signs of His return is that
the gospel message would be preached as a witness to all people groups and then He would return. What a glorious hope!
Christ has said that He will return when the task of evangelizing the world is complete. In one sense, we may, in God's
sovereign plan, hasten that day by our active participation
in God's global outreach. So, based on the Lord's promise to
us, we keep busy, we exhort the peoples to worship the living
God, we pray that God would be praised among the nations,
and we work together as God's representatives to make His
greatness known. To what end? Note in Revelation what John
saw as he indicates the presence of all peoples in heaven:

> *After these things, I looked, and behold, a great mul-*
> *titude, which no one could count, from every nation*
> *and all tribes and peoples and tongues, standing be-*
> *fore the throne and before the Lamb, clothed in white*
> *robes, and palm branches were in their hands; and they*
> *cry out with a loud voice, saying, "Salvation belongs*
> *to our God, who sits on he throne, and to the Lamb.*[20]

The plan has always been, therefore, that people from all
the nations of the earth would come to know the name of the
Lord, the essence of His character, and the blessings of His
deeds of grace, mercy, and salvation, the message of which
would be borne by His people throughout the ages.

Conclusion

Scripture provides many helpful insights to be considered and reconsidered regarding the mission of the Church. The mission of the Church, as noted above, is to take part in God's mission by (1) going throughout the world as God's ambassadors, with the authority of Jesus, to bear witness to Jesus Christ and who He is and also to make disciples; (2) loving God and neighbor; (3) making a difference in the world by being agents of change (salt and light); (4) praying for more workers (ministry leaders, pastors, missionaries) to be raised up, trained, and sent out; (5) living the missional lifestyle (as Paul did); and (6) worshiping God and making other worshipers.

Suggested Resources

Walter C. Kaiser, Jr. *Mission in the Old Testament: Israel as a Light to the Nations.* Grand Rapids: Baker Books, 2000.

Andreas J. Kostenberger and Peter T. O'Brien. *Salvation to the Ends of the Earth: A Biblical Theology of Mission.* Downers Grove: InterVarsity Press, 2001.

William J. Larkin, Jr. and Joel F. Williams, eds. *Mission in the New Testament: An Evangelical Approach.* Maryknoll, NY: Orbis Books, 1998.

John Piper. *Let the Nations Be Glad!: The Supremacy of God in Missions*, 2nd ed. Grand Rapids: Baker Books, 2003.

Ralph D. Winter and Steven C. Hawthorne, eds. *Perspectives on the World Christian Movement: A Reader.* 4th ed. Pasadena: William Carey Library, 2009.

Christopher J.H. Wright. *The Mission of God: Unlocking the Bible's Grand Narrative.* Downers Grove: IVP Academic, 2006.

Notes

[1] Leonidas A. Johnson, *The African American Church: Waking Up to God's Missionary Call* (Pasadena: William Carey Library, 2006), 3.

[2] John R.W. Stott, "The Bible in World Evangelization," in *Perspectives on the World Christian Movement*, 4th ed., ed. Ralph D. Winter and Steven C. Hawthorne (Pasadena: William Carey Library, 2009), 21-26.

[3] See Genesis 1-11, Exodus 22:21, Leviticus 19:33-34, Deuteronomy 10:17-19, 28:7-14, 2 Samuel 7:8-16, 1 Kings 8:22-53, 2 Chronicles 6:32-33, Psalms 96, 105, 117, Isaiah 6:1-13, 9:2, 42:6, 49:6, Ezekiel 1-3, the book of Daniel, Amos 9:12, the book of Jonah, Zechariah 2:11, 14:9, and Malachi 1:11. Note also the various non-Israelites (i.e., Gentiles) who are mentioned in the Old Testament that also had some kind of relationship with God—Melchizedek (Genesis 14:18-20), Jethro (Exodus 2:16, 3:1), Rahab (Joshua 2; cf. Hebrews 11:31), and Ruth (Ruth 1:16).

[4] Walter C. Kaiser, Jr., "Israel's Missionary Call," in *Perspectives on the World Christian Movement*, 4th ed., ed. Ralph D. Winter and Steven C. Hawthorne (Pasadena: William Carey Library, 2009), 10-16.

[5] Writer and social thinker Amy Sherman describes it this way, "The invitation to join God in his work in the world continues in what we might label the Great Call in Genesis 12:1-3. At this point in the Great Narrative of Scripture, the world has collapsed into ruin as a result of the Fall. But God has a magnificent plan for redemption and restoration...[The] *missio Dei* is the sending love of God poured into the world to bring about restoration of all that was lost in the Fall: peace with God, peace with self, peace with others, and peace with creation. And God decides to use a human family, Abraham's, as a vehicle through which he will work. In Genesis 12, God promises to bless Abraham and make him a blessing to all the peoples on the earth." (Amy Sherman, "Made for Work", in *The Pastor's Guide to Fruitful Work & Economic Wisdom: Understanding What Your People Do All Day*, ed. Drew Cleveland and Greg Forster (Overland Park, KS: Made to Flourish, 2012), 26.

[6]John Piper, *Let the Nations Be Glad!: The Supremacy of God in Missions*, 2nd ed. (Grand Rapids: Baker Books, 2003), 169.

[7]Piper, *Let the Nations Be Glad!*, 174.

[8]Walter C. Kaiser, Jr., *Mission in the Old Testament: Israel as a Light to the Nations* (Grand Rapids: Baker Books, 2000), 20.

[9]George Peters, *A Biblical Theology of Missions* (Chicago: Moody, 1972), 115-116; quoted in Ibid., 29.

[10]As Old Testament scholar Derek Kidner notes, the "spirit of the psalm . . . is that of the Abrahamic hope." (Derek Kidner, *Psalms: An Introduction and Commentary on Books I and II of the Psalms*, 2 vols. (Downers Grove: InterVarsity Press, 1973), 236.

[11]Kaiser, *Mission in the Old Testament*, 32.

[12]It has been consistently demonstrated elsewhere by various New Testament scholars that the original manuscripts probably did not contain these verses and were added at a later point by the early Church. This issue will not be taken up here, as the content of these verses are consistent with the other gospel accounts and with the other recorded teachings of Jesus.

[13]John Stott, *Romans: God's Good News for the World* (Downers Grove: InterVarsity Press, 1994), 286.

[14]John Calvin, *Calvin's Commentaries, Volume XIX: Acts 14-28, Romans 1-16* (1540, 1552; reprint, Grand Rapids: Wm. B. Eerdmans Publishing Company, 1993), 399.

[15]Note further in verses 23ff his plans to continue his international ministry beyond what he had already done to that point.

[16]New Testament scholar P.T. O'Brien proposes another insight into Paul's version of the Great Commission. In his book, *Gospel and Mission in the Writings of Paul*, O'Brien suggests from Ephesians 6:10-20 that evangelism and making disciples, which is empowered by God's Spirit, is part of the spiritual war that Christians find themselves in. Obeying the Great Commission, then, means taking up the offensive by advancing on the enemy's territory, resisting his attacks and pro-

claiming the good news of the gospel to those being held in captivity (P.T. O'Brien, *Gospel and Mission in the Writings of Paul: An Exegetical and Theological Analysis* (Grand Rapids: Baker Books, 1995).

[17] I. Howard Marshall, *I Peter* (Downers Grove: InterVarsity Press, 1991), 74.

[18] Recall here that Jesus Himself invested the Church with God's authority as He commissioned and sent His people into the world to make disciples (see Matthew 28:18-20).

[19] Piper, *Let the Nations Be Glad!*, 170-174. See, for example, Psalms 66:1-4, 86:8-10, 96:1-10, Isaiah 12, Jeremiah 16:19-21, Zephaniah 3:8-12, and Malachi 1:11.

[20] Revelation 7:9-10 (NASB); cf. Revelation 5:9, 14:6-7, 15:3-4, 21:24 & 26, and 22:2.

CHAPTER 3

MISSIONS AWARENESS AND EDUCATION

"God has called us into this world to be His lights and witnesses, and we choose to make His world a focus of our attention. His global concerns are our priorities, and we surround ourselves with reminders of His world perspective."[1]

- Paul Borthwick -

"The missions addiction consumes me. The fire in me is no longer fueled by youth. Now it is fueled by truth."[2]

- David Shibley -

"Hi, my name is Rich, and I am addicted to missions."

It is a healthy addiction from which I do not need deliverance; I also have not elevated it to a place where the mission is more important than God. That would make it an idol. Granted, I love to travel, and I love interacting with different cultures, but most of all I love God.

When I am doing my part to know Him better, I am more aware of His love consuming me and I find that my heart starts beating with His heart, and His heart beats for the peoples of this world, with whom He desires to be in relationship. Then the need to truly love others gets intensified and I am compelled to tell people of the living God and His incredible love for us. But I'm not satisfied until I'm also inviting others into the same level of awareness of, passion for, and commitment to the *missio Dei* as people living on mission together in this world.

Living this way, as God's people, includes having a collective, church-wide enthusiastic commitment to missions and to what God is doing all around the world. Every local church should work very hard to foster such a global interest within the hearts of their people. God's mission ought to be seen as the priority and focus of all church ministry. A missional climate should, therefore, be developed within every congregation as the "mission" is integrated into every ministry program of the church, as expressed locally, regionally, and globally. People, especially young people, should be confronted with their responsibility to evangelize the people of this generation around the world while being challenged to see where they fit into God's global plan.

If our spiritual forefathers and foremothers had not done this, we would likely not be here today. The Church of Jesus Christ and countless millions would have died without a knowledge of Jesus Christ or the way to salvation. The people with whom we share life, wherever they live in this world, need us to live as if what we believe really matters. If the people of this world are ever going to hear the good news of the gospel, we are the ones who get the bring it to them. The *missio Dei* should, therefore, be fully integrated into our way of life as followers of Jesus.

How does this happen? How can we do this in our churches? How can we influence others in our churches to get on board with what God is doing? Missions expert Paul Borthwick suggests that the "best missions awareness in a youth ministry occurs when a group (and the leaders) are consistently thinking about evangelism, discipleship, and the fulfillment of the Great Commission. A one-time spurt of missions involvement may make us feel like 'world Christian' youth leaders, but a *year-round missions education* will produce the best long-term results."[3] Borthwick writes in terms of mobilizing teenagers for missions, but the same is true for any age. Missions awareness and education needs to happen consistently throughout the year as the life-giving heartbeat of the church. What follows are some suggestions to help the local church do that very thing.

Missions Mobilization Team

To be successful in this venture will require someone besides the pastor or missions pastor to take the lead. Regardless of size, every local church should have a Missions Mobilization Team (MMT) or Missions Committee in place to help provide leadership in the area of generating missions awareness throughout the year. This team should meet regularly throughout the year to work together to keep the mission before the congregation.[4] On the surface, the work of the MMT may seem daunting. It doesn't have to be this way, though. One of the things I have learned in my years of ministry experience as a pastor and missions leader is the principle of intentional simplicity—keep things focused, consistent, and intentional, based on the needs and desires of the congregation, while doing things as simply as possible. For example, if your church is on the smaller side, it will likely be better to plan a weekend missions event that fits the family-like dynamics of the congregation rather than trying to pull off a week (or even an entire month) full of big activities that are designed for larger groups. Keeping it simple, consistent, and intentional will be more meaningful and have a greater impact than trying to do too much with too little.

General Functions of the Missions Mobilization Team. What does the MMT do? Broadly speaking, these leaders assist the pastor in casting vision, establishing a strategy, and setting goals for missions and cross-cultural ministry in the church while also helping to create missions awareness by promoting the cause of worldwide evangelization and disciple-making in the church. This process of creating missions awareness includes:

- Plan and oversee at least one missions event (e.g. a missions conference) per year, as well as other missions awareness events
- Stimulate prayer for missionaries and their ministry, as well as for the evangelization and discipling of the people of the world and other missions-related items
- Educate the church regarding what the Bible says about missions and what missions is
- Build a resource library of missions-related books, magazines, and videos
- Promote, plan and oversee short-term missions experiences, cross-cultural ministry partnerships, and

ministries to internationals living in the church's community

- Oversee care ministry to missionaries sent from or related to the church
- Help the pastor, elders, and other relevant church leaders establish policies related to cross-cultural ministry efforts of the church
- Assist the pastor, elders, and other relevant church leaders establish goals for giving financially to missions and help administer missions-related budget items and financial obligations
- Lead the people of the congregation by example

For insights on how these things may be carried out, please refer to the chapters that follow.

Missions Mobilization Team (MMT) Membership & Responsibilities. In my opinion, the MMT should consist of no more than fourteen people, depending on church size and needs, so that each of the ministry areas addressed below is provided for. In a small congregation, which has usually been my experience as both a layperson and a pastor, the MMT might only have a few members who serve in multiple roles simultaneously.[5] Ultimately, then, it is not the size of the team that matters as much as work that the team does.

Ideally, the MMT consists of at least the following members: The Team Leader, The Secretary, The Missions Prayer Coordinator, The Missions Education Coordinator, The Teen Representative, The Missionary Treasurer, a representative from women's and/or men's denominational missions-focused organizations, and The Senior/Staff Pastor. For a description of each of these positions, as well as ideas for other positions, please refer to Appendix A.

Missions Mobilization Team Member Characteristics and Expectations. MMT members will each have a personal relationship with Jesus, being dedicated to serving Him in all areas of life and being devoted to prayer as the first work in all ministry. They will have a passion for evangelizing and making disciples of people from all cultures all over the world, including the church's local community. They should demonstrate a commitment to local, regional, and global outreach ministry. They will have a heart to see others mobilized for cross-cultural ministry around the world, with a desire to serve in missions-related leadership in the local church. They will be team players who give sacrificially of their time, talents, and treasure while showing leadership skills with an ability to properly administrate things. Finally, if the church is part of a denominational family, they will be committed to the work of their denominational missionaries and ministries, even while maintaining a Kingdom of God mindset that celebrates and participates in what God is doing through all denominational and parachurch organizational work.

MMT members are also expected to commit to serving for a full term (either one, two, or three years; renewable), attend all MMT meetings, lead an MMT sub-committee on an as-needed basis, attend at least one missions training event per year, and commit to continue to learn about missions and missions practice to help keep their heart and mind focused while remaining aware of missions trends and strategies.

The Missions Conference

Church missions conferences are normal for me. I grew up in churches that held them and they always served as good reminders for the church to stay involved with missions. For many denominations, such as the one in which I serve, annual missions conferences are expected. For other denominations and churches, though, this concept is less familiar. Because of my own experience and knowing the experiences of countless other churches of various denominations and affiliations, I believe it would be good for churches to conduct at least one missions conference each year, as well as other missions mobilization events. Why? The short answer is because it is key to keeping God's work around the world in front of the congregation.

The long answer includes the following reasons. First, missionaries are given the opportunity to report to the Church what the Lord is doing in their part of the world through their ministries, just as the Apostle Paul and Barnabas did (see Acts 15:3-4). The conference, then, functions like a stakeholders' meeting. The people we invest in report on how that investment is working out, allowing us to celebrate God's faithfulness together. Second, those uninterested in missions have an opportunity to become interested as they see God at work. Third, people are reminded of their personal involvement and investment in the Great Commission through praying, giving, going, and sending. As a result, intercession for lost people around the world is renewed and giving to missions is increased as people recommit to seeing God's work accomplished.

Does it have to be called "Missions Conference"? No. In fact, be creative about what to call it. Here are some ideas: Annual Missions Conference, Global Awareness Weekend/ Week, Global Focus, Global Celebration (Weekend/Week), Missions Fest, World Fest, Missions Celebration Weekend/ Week, Missions Emphasis Weekend/Week, or Global Impact.

How often should a church have a missions conference? Many churches find it helpful to have one in the fall and one in the spring, for either a weekend or a full week in each of those seasons. Many pastors and missions mobilization teams also take advantage of inviting various missionaries and international visitors to speak at small groups, worship services, or other events when they are in the area. Another idea is to have short-term missionaries or short-term missions teams that are part of the church share about their ministry involvement. You don't have to be a megachurch to do this. Any size church can do a missions conference and do it well. All that's needed is some leadership, some planning, and some intentionality to pay attention for opportunities.

How long should such a conference last? That is up to the appropriate church leadership as they decide what the needs and desires are for the congregation. Some churches commit to a week-long conference that involves a lot of activities, ranging from special worship services to missions-focused prayer gatherings to church family time with the missionaries to missionaries spending time with select segments of the congregation. Other churches do *some* of those things over the course of a weekend. Still other churches, often the larger congregations, decide to commit an entire month to missions. The point is not how long a conference should last, or even how often (beyond once a year). The point is that it happens in a way that is in alignment with the personae of the church and relevant to their ministry.

For a successful conference or event, I think that two planning teams are most beneficial: a Creative Thinking Team and a Program Team. Both of these teams could function as one team and could be a sub-committee of the Missions Mobilization Team or could be the actual MMT. Each team should together meet to discuss the conference or event theme (which is often times predetermined for denominational churches) and establish some basic goals and outcomes for the conference or event and how that fits in with the overall missional focus of the church; meetings should start happening no later than two-three months prior to the conference.

The *Creative Thinking Team* is made up of the people who are creative visionaries. They come up with the ideas but don't necessarily put them into practice, so they pass these ideas on to the Program Team. If there is only one team, whether a sub-committee or the MMT, have the creative people on the team brainstorm the ideas. This team should not only generate ideas but should also assist the Program Team in planning and carrying out the conference, particularly in the area of promotion.

The *Program Team* consists of the administrative type of people who may or may not develop creative ideas but certainly make sure ideas come to fruition. This team provides the administrative planning aspect to conference planning that makes sure everything happens the way it's supposed to. If there is only one team, whether a sub-committee or the MMT, empower the administrative people carry out the implementation of ideas, possibly with the assistance of the Creative Thinking Team. Specific duties of the Program Team include the following:

- Pray for the conference/event before it begins, while it is happening, and after it ends and encourage the congregation to pray as well.
- Work with the pastor to determine church-wide meeting times and occasions.
- Decide the dates, times, and places of various meetings, as well as what will happen at each event (based on needs and interests of the various age groups).
- Determine travel and housing arrangements for each participating missionary.

- Communicate (early and often) with each missionary that will be participating via phone or email. Inquire about their interests and desires; confirm the schedule, housing arrangements, dietary needs, and transportation issues.
- Promote the conference or event (see Promotional Ideas below).
- Decorate the church facilities accordingly.
- Help the pastor identify a goal for missions giving.
- Assist the pastor (or worship pastor) in planning a worship service or services during the conference. Help with song selections, special music possibilities, drama presentation possibilities, etc.
- Plan effectively for any events involving food.
- Build a timeline for the event, which can maximize planning efforts.

To get missions conference activities that have been tested and used by various churches that I have been a part of or have interacted with, check out Appendix B, where you will also find a list of conference promotional ideas to assist with your planning.

Basic Missions Promotion

Although missions conferences are key pieces to the promotion of missions year-round, it will take more than one such event to keep missions in front of the congregation. Here are some ideas to get you thinking.

Moment for Missions. One of the easiest and most common ways of keeping missions in front of people is to include a regular missions update within worship services, at least once per month. By design, these updates are short and strategically placed within the order of worship. If you choose to do this, it can be done in a variety of ways, from people sharing a testimony or reading a missionary's newsletter or email update to quick phone interviews with missionaries to using videos and PowerPoint presentations. Each update could then be followed with a brief prayer that focuses on the nature of the update. The key here is to regularly provide updates to the congregation in a creative, personal, and relevant way. Updates may also be incorporated in Sunday school classes and small group meetings. In the church where I recently served as senior pastor, we did this twice each month, with one Sunday focusing on the local or regional expression of the mission, and one Sunday focusing on the global expression. There are churches of all sizes that only do this once per month, while others do it every Sunday.

Use the Worship Bulletin and Newsletter. Regularly include information about missions and missionaries in the worship service bulletin and church's newsletter (if the church has one). If space is an issue, you could at least identify international workers to pray for during the coming week. In the churches I have pastored, we have always highlighted one to three missionaries each week in the bulletin. These are missionaries who the church is somehow directly affiliated with or personally know, or who are associated with our denominational region. This helps to keep things personal and relational. People tend to pray more for people they know. This has always been warmly received by these congregations and missionaries that we know feel all the more supported and are often likely to share more personal notes of news and prayer items. Many churches that I know of, both denominational and non-denominational, have similar practices.

Use the Church's Website. If your church has a website, here are some things you can include on it: information about the church's missions-related ministries and activities; missions-related prayer requests; missions-related resources; missions videos; links to denomination-related missions ministries; links to websites of missionaries related to the church; and links to missions resource agencies like Frontier Ventures (formerly the U.S. Center for World Mission). A note of caution here as it relates to posting information about some missionaries. Many do work in "creative access" areas where it is difficult and dangerous to be a Christian or do to Christian ministry, so please respect security guidelines and any pleas for privacy that are made by a missionary. Many denominations and missions sending agencies have such guidelines already established and should be consulted. A quick survey of church websites—of churches of all sizes—will reveal some great examples of this type of missions awareness.

Use the Arts. There are many missions-related works of art that are available for a church to use in promoting global awareness, including music, music videos, movies, drama, painting, photography, dance, banners, poetry, dramatic storytelling, multi-media presentations, and even food. Consider hosting music concerts or an arts festival that feature a missions theme. Maybe have a missions movie night. Perhaps incorporate occasional skits in the worship services or host a missions-themed dramatic presentation, or even produce your own. If there are artists in the church, encourage them to use their creative gifts, talents and abilities in telling God's story and using their art to communicate missions. This is an area that is often overlooked, but I have personally seen the arts begin to have a voice in this arena and have heard similar stories from around the United States, Canada, Europe, Africa, and the Middle East.

Regular Missions Education

The process of getting a church excited about missions, as well as the very task of world evangelization and disciplemaking, is incomplete without solid instruction and preparation. Just as it is important to foster a global awareness in the church, so it is important to have a basic level of education about missions throughout the year. Such education includes foundational instruction in the Bible, basic theology, and missions, as well as ministry skill development so that people may be prepared to serve the Lord for a lifetime. For churches that are committed to equipping people in worship services, Sunday school classes, one-on-one discipleship opportunities, and various kinds of small groups, there are many resources available, including books, missions-focused curriculum, seminars and workshops, training events, conferences, classes, and the Internet.

There are three key ways to do this. First, *be informed.* One way to be informed is to stay up to date with current events and ministry reports that come from missionaries so that you know what is happening around the world. Another way is to do basic research to learn about the countries and regions where missionaries serve, where unreached and least-reached people groups live, and where persecution of Christians is occurring.[6] It is also helpful to learn from missionaries of the past, to know their stories of how they heard from God and were compelled to take the gospel message to the ends of the earth. In the end, being informed is about paying attention to what God has done and is doing locally, regionally, and globally, both within and outside of your denominational affiliation.

The second key way to educate people about missions is to *make resources available* to people who like to read, as well as to teachers, small group leaders, and small group partici-pants. These days, it is easy to make use of the Internet and to strategically leverage social media and various forms of print media for this purpose. I want to also suggest that you estab-lish a missions library at your church, a library that contains books about missions theology and missions history, as well as biographies and autobiographies of missionaries, missions promotional materials, and missions curricula for Sunday school classes and small groups.

Finally, *creatively educate* people. Teach them what the Bible says about missions, basic theology, and the history of missions. For younger generations, approaching this in an ac-tive and experiential manner is particularly important. This can be done by making effective use of Sunday school classes, small groups, and children and youth ministry meetings while also conducting, hosting, or attending regional events that are designed to expose, motivate, and equip people for ministry and missions.

Spiritual Formation

Spiritual formation is another extremely important part of generating missions awareness and educating others about missional living. This essentially means helping people rec-ognize that when we live in a way that moves us into deep-er relationship with Jesus, a growing vitality develops within this relationship that produces within us a greater passion for Him and for serving Him. When this relationship is in place, things like missions and reaching the lost are an automatic by-product as our heart beats with God's heart. When we love God and pursue intimacy with Christ, we are compelled to love people and to share God's story of love and grace with them. As Ken Uyeda Fong notes, this kind of "spiritual renew-al will create an intense desire to be a more integral part of the

Savior's will and work in the world. It leads to the renewal of the vision for the mission of the church."[7] So, as we mature in our faith as people who love and serve Jesus, ministry will naturally (or supernaturally) come, and we will passionately desire to serve Him wherever He leads, including the other side of the world.

People who live in a consumer-driven and impatient culture (like the one I live in), need help in understanding that growing spiritually in this way is a lifelong process that is ultimately focused around a relationship with Jesus. This process takes time and there is nothing pre-packaged about it. There are no simple and effective formulaic spirituality programs or "how-to" manuals outside of the Bible. So, as we invest in people and help them become more missionally aware, we can begin by assisting them in this process of spiritual growth. As such, let me suggest four significant ways that we can go about this: (1) encourage people to go deeper in their relationship with God through Jesus Christ, (2) exhort them to love God more and know Christ more intimately each day, (3) inspire them to live the Christ life and a life of progressive holiness where new life in Christ continues to develop and the old life of sin is consistently conquered, and (4) instruct people to be filled with the Holy Spirit, relying fully on Him to sanctify and empower them.

Included within this spiritual formation process is the element of sacrifice. Therefore, people who desire to follow Jesus should also be: (1) gently reminded that loving God and following Jesus include times of struggle, pain, disappointment, and personal sacrifice, (2) confronted with what it means to submit totally to the lordship of Jesus Christ and whether or not they are willing to lose everything for the sake of following Him, and (3) motivated to abandon the pursuit of what this world offers in order to surrender fully to Christ by dying to the world with its affections and desires. After all, attempting to live as Jesus lived takes account of the realization that changing the world involves a level of sacrifice. As this occurs, a better understanding and acceptance of life on the mission field will be generated.

Knowing this, may we then realize that many people, especially members of the younger generations, are longing to be fulfilled at the spiritual level and will do anything to satisfy this need. We should challenge them to go deeper in their faith through preaching, teaching, Bible study, and being a living witness; we should encourage them to count the cost of following and serving Jesus.[8] We can do this by creating the kind of atmosphere for spiritual formation to occur, where a passion for God and for serving Him is cultivated. This atmosphere can occur within worship experiences, small groups, or one-on-one discussions, for instance. We can also encourage people to do their part in maintaining their relationship with God through spiritual habits such as Bible reading and studying, prayer, and worship. Finally, we can pray for one another's spiritual growth and vitality as we live on mission together.

A Missional Climate

A vision for missions—for being on mission together—includes having a knowledge of, a passion for, and a commitment to, what God is doing around the world. If we want to see our churches see missions as more than just an occasional ministry or thing that we do, then creating and sustaining a missional climate where the *missio Dei* is part of everything that we do is a top priority. May it be so in your life and in your church; may it be so in mine.

Principle in Practice

Promote, Report, and Celebrate

Valley Community Baptist Church is a large, multi-site church in Avon, Connecticut and other nearby communities. In all their locations, they are very intentional to keep the focus on missions alive and well. When you look on their website, this becomes very clear–they are committed to "actively reach out to [their] neighbors in the local community and beyond, even to some of the world's most remote and impoverished areas." With a very supportive senior pastor, Valley's missions strategy includes extensive prayer for missions (the primary part of this strategy), generous giving to the work of missions, short-term missions involvement, and long-term investment via strong partnerships with missionaries.

Another important aspect of their strategy is seen in how the World Outreach Committee of fifteen people keeps the community aware of and educated about missions. But it's not their work alone. There are also sixty-five other world outreach leaders that serve on sub-committees to help with the work of this ministry. Throughout the year this group of leaders and missions enthusiasts work hard to do such things as carry out the annual spring "World Outreach Week" missions conference that highlights the church's local, regional, and global mission involvement while inviting people to participate in the annual faith-promise missions budget.

Doug Christgau, Valley's Pastor of Outreach, says that the "calling card" of this weeklong event is their "World Outreach Tour," which consists of three decorated, interactive missionary stations that connect the week's theme with missionaries who are speaking that week. Around 1,000 people end up passing through these stations, and they follow this up with an action station where people can respond in a variety of ways. Each November also features a missions weekend event that serves the same purposes. These world outreach leaders also conduct ten missions prayer partner luncheons with supported missionaries, connect each of the church's weekly adult Bible study fellowships with a missionary, make sure the church's website contains missions highlights and outreach ministry opportunities, prepare missions-related announcement slides for worship gatherings, keep their "Agape Hallway" updated with recent photos of and information about supported missionaries and teams, and maintain the world outreach screen that features videos or brief video presentations about missions and supported missionaries that are played in facility common areas during weekend services and midweek programs.

This all may seem daunting for smaller congregations, but Christgau maintains that any size church, even small ones, "can promote, report, and celebrate what God is doing around the world."

A Longstanding Commitment to Missions

East Main Presbyterian (ECO) Church in the small town of Grove City, Pennsylvania, is a medium-sized church that, according to their website, "has a longstanding commitment to mission," as seen in their devotion to mission partnerships and personal involvement of the people in various kinds of missional ministry opportunities throughout the community and around the world. This time-honored dedication is there in part because of three significant voices (an interim pastor and two laypeople) in the history of the church who left their deep imprint by helping to develop missions principles for the congregation while making sure that missions remained a focus.

Several years ago, the church's missions committee was challenged by their pastor at the time to remember this commitment and this heritage. Karen Campbell and her missions committee of twelve people are passionately devoted to "doing what they can to keep missions in front of people." They work hard to keep the people aware of missions, to connect them to the twenty-or-so missionaries (not all of whom are Presbyterian) they support around the world, and to help organize and facilitate ministry experiences locally, regionally, and globally.

Awareness happens through the committee's efforts to include up-to-date missionary and missions organization information and prayer requests in worship service bulletins, on church bulletin boards, and on the church's website, as well has presenting a "minute for missions" once per month within their main worship gathering. They are also doing things like missions emphasis Sundays every other year, where people are encouraged to regularly pray for and give to the work of missions; special offerings for missions and supported missionaries also happen three times each year. Of course, when missionaries are in town, they are also given time to preach and/or share reports in worship services and other gatherings—a great way to maintain and strengthen the relationships that exist.

Two other things that East Main does are especially noteworthy: involving the children of the congregation and setting up an annual Christmas Mission Market. East Main recognizes the importance of starting to expose people to missions early on. Children are always invited to participate, and each children's Sunday school class has adopted and befriended a missionary to pray for and encourage. The Christmas Market is designed to bless missionaries and their families with specific projects that they have. With various needs identified, the "market" goes into action as people of all ages, especially families, excitedly receive missionaries' "shopping lists" and give toward these projects, no matter how big or small the project is and no matter how much money an individual or family is able to give. Along the way, people learn more about these missionaries through the information and pictures that are on display at the church during the Christmas season.

Karen's wisdom for other churches? "Don't let lack of money keep you from doing missions awareness. Not much money is needed to do this."

Suggested Resources

Paul Borthwick. *A Mind for Missions*. Colorado Springs: Navpress, 1987.

Paul Borthwick. *How to Be a World-Class Christian*. Wheaton: Victor Books, 1991.

Carl F. Ellis, Jr. *Going Global Beyond the Boundaries: The Role of the Black Church in the Great Commission of Jesus Christ*. Chicago: Urban Ministries, Inc., 2005.

Frontier Ventures. *Perspectives on the World Christian Movement* course (information at www.frontierventures.org/ministries/perspectives)

David Mays. *Stuff You Need to Know About Missions in Your Church, Vols. 1-5*. (information & availability at http://davidmays.org/Resources/resmays.html)

David Mays. *Becoming a World-Changing Church*. 2010. (available at http://davidmays.org/Becoming.pdf)

David Mays. *The Mission Leadership Team: Mobilizing Your Church to Touch the World*. Stone Mountain, GA: The Mission Exchange, 2010.

Ruth A. Tucker. *From Jerusalem to Irian Jaya: A Biographical History of Christian Missions*. 2nd ed. Grand Rapids: Zondervan, 2004.

David and Lorene Wilson, eds. *Pipeline: Engaging the Church in Missionary Mobilization*. Littleton: William Carey Press, 2018.

Ralph D. Winter and Steven C. Hawthorne, eds. *Perspectives on the World Christian Movement: A Reader*. 4th ed. Pasadena: William Carey Library, 2009.

Notes

[1] Paul Borthwick, *A Mind for Missions* (Colorado Springs: Navpress, 1987), 150.

[2] David Shibley, *The Missions Addiction* (Lake Mary, FL: Charisma House, 2001), 231.

[3] Paul Borthwick, *Youth and Missions*, 2nd ed. (Waynesboro, GA: OM Literature, 1998), 99-100. (emphasis added)

[4] For some churches, meeting regularly translates into once per month. For others, it means meeting 4-6 times per year. How often the team meets depends on who is on the team and what the needs of the church are as it relates to missions awareness.

[5] My friend is part of a small church in Beaver Falls, PA, and he once remarked to me that suggesting a committee of fourteen in a church his size would be about one-third of the congregation. That is an observation that I and so many others can really resonate with.

[6] See Appendix C, "Responding to the Persecuted Church," for some further insight here.

[7] Ken Uyeda Fong, *Pursuing the Pearl: A Comprehensive Resource for Multi-Asian Ministry* (Valley Forge: Judson Press, 1999), 178.

[8] Studies have consistently shown that Millennials, and now also Generation Z, are willing to take this journey with all its demands and that they will make total life commitments to a cause or a person (in this case, Jesus Christ). They just need to be inspired and challenged to do it, rather than just be entertained by the typical youth ministry program.

CHAPTER 4

PRAYING FOR MISSIONS AND MISSIONARIES

"Reaching the nations of the world requires that we are people of prayer. For it is out of an intimate walk with God that the church is filled with the Spirit to carry out the Great Commission."[1]

- J.D. Payne -

"It is a mystery that our loving Father has somehow limited His omnipotence to partner with His redeemed people so that His actions in the world are inextricably linked with our prayers...The nations are there for the asking. God is calling you and me into the ministry of intercession for them."[2]

- Jason Mandryk -

Around 30 years ago, I was struck by a mission's agency bro-chure that encouraged people to pray for missionaries and their ministry. What got my attention then that still capti-vates me today was their tagline: "Most Christians believe in the importance of prayer, but missionaries survive by it."

Let that sink in for a moment. Now take another moment to begin unpacking the implications of such a statement. I don't remember the name of the agency, but their tagline was powerful enough that it still resonates with me today, and it serves as an important reminder of how incredibly vital the ministry of prayer is. In fact, it should be our top priority, just as it was for Jesus Himself. Prayer should take precedence in all that is done. It should be the first work in all things since the Church, like Jesus, trusts God for everything. This is true for life, for local church ministry of all kinds, and for missions.

As it relates to praying for God's work around the world, there are some helpful preliminary thoughts to con-sider from John Piper's message "Prayer: The Work of Mis-sions," presented at the 1988 annual meeting of Advancing Churches in Missions Commitment (ACMC).[3] In this mes-sage, Piper says,

> In order to mobilize a movement of prayer in the church and in order to sustain a will to pray in our hearts, we must think and talk about other things besides prayer. This is the key lesson I have learned in recent years.

1. We must talk first about war. Because life is war. And it is utterly impossible for people to know what prayer really is until they know that they are in a war, and until they know that the stakes of that war are in-finitely higher than the stakes in [any human war we may be involved with].

2. We must talk about the Sovereignty of God. Because only from this great truth can we know that we will win the war. And only then will we have hope and strength to press on in a life of prayer.

3. Then, when we have spoken first about the war we are in and next about the sovereignty of God, then we can come to what I will call the awesome place of prayer in God's purposes for the world.

Missions expert Paul Borthwick further provides some helpful advice when it comes to praying for missions. In his book *How to Be a World-Class Christian*, Borthwick suggests three ways to pray: manageably, practically, and strategically. To pray *manageably* means to pray for people we know and world events that we are personally aware of, realizing that it's too overwhelming to try to pray for everything. To pray *practically* means praying for those needs that we are personally aware of, while also being sensitive to how the Holy Spirit may further direct our prayers. This will come from our personal and church connections with missionaries and particular mission fields. To pray *strategically* means to pray for government leaders to create situations that will expedite ministry efforts rather than hinder them, and to pray for national church leaders and international workers who minister alongside them.[5]

Encouraging Missions-Related Prayer

As mentioned, prayer should be a personal and a corporate priority in all that we do. In our churches, then, we ought to regularly pray for missions and missionaries when we gather together in worship, in Sunday school classes, and in small groups. Here is where a good Missions Prayer Coordinator comes in to lead and encourage missions prayer efforts by making prayer needs known to the church family in various ways.

Here are some ideas to help connect congregants in the pew with God's work around the world.

Help People Visualize. Keeping the work of missions prominently displayed goes a long way in helping people to see what God is doing among the nations and peoples of this world. One way to do this is to highlight mission fields and missionaries to pray for in the worship service bulletin and during pre-worship service presentation slides (when applicable) each week, particularly those fields or workers that your church may be associated with in some way. You could also assemble a missions prayer booklet that highlights missionaries, countries, or projects that are related to the church through membership or denomination.

Helping people in this way can also include prominently displaying a map of the world that highlights where missionaries and missions projects are (particularly those missionaries and projects that are directly connected with the church), or perhaps pictures of people and projects related to your missionaries or your direct involvement as visual reminders of the mission.

Keep People Informed. If we want people to pray then it is helpful to let them know how to pray and what to pray for. This can be done by posting or distributing a page of missions-related prayer requests each week. Sometimes denominations or associations makes such requests available, making our work of gathering and disseminating such information even easier. Of course, when we receive prayer updates and newsletters from missionaries and missions ministries with whom we are connected, we can easily post or distribute them as well. Also, if the church facility has a prayer room, you could devote one wall to be the "international" wall where missions-related prayer needs can be regularly posted and updated.

Other ways to inform people include developing and using missions-only email and social media prayer chains, posting current missions-related prayer requests on the church website,[6] encouraging use of prayer guides like *Operation World* or *Pray for the World* or guides put together by your denomination or association, and encouraging use of prayer smartphone apps like "JP Unreached" and "Operation World," highlighting international current events and crises from the pulpit, and actively working to remember our persecuted brothers and sisters in Christ around the world.

Provide People with Opportunities. Aside from inviting people to pray during corporate worship experiences, there are two other opportunities that we can make available to people. One thing we can do is establish some small groups where people meet specifically and solely to pray for missionaries and missions. Another option is to conduct regular concerted prayer gatherings for missions.

How to Pray

It's easy to encourage and inspire people to pray. Many people, though, fall a little short in this area because they may not know how to pray or what to pray for; at best, their prayers are very generalized. I admit that sometimes I am guilty of this. I find it very helpful, then, to have lists of specific items to be praying for, and I know many others who feel the same way. Not only am I more informed and strategic with my prayers, but I'm also deepening my relationship with my heavenly Father as we talk together about important matters. I also strengthen my relationship with missionaries as they share their life with me via their prayer requests. Knowing that many of us approach intercession for others in this way, it may be helpful to share Borthwick's ten suggested steps (mentioned above), as well as the ideas that follow here, with people to help get them started in this important ministry.

Perspective. When praying, it is best to begin by praising God for who He is and what He has done. It is also good to thank Him for how He has specifically answered prayers that were previously offered. This helps put things in proper perspective as we remember that it's never about us. Rather, it is always about Him.

Countries, Regions, and People Groups. When thinking of the world, prayer can be offered for people all over the earth—especially unreached and least-reached people groups—to be reached with the gospel of Jesus Christ and for churches to be established among them. In the last few decades there has been much emphasis on the "10/40 Window" as the main place where unreached and least-reached people live, but more recently there has been a renewed emphasis on the reality that there are other spiritually dark places in the world as well. The acronym "T.H.U.M.B." is a useful tool used by many people and missions organizations to keep this perspective, as it helps us simply remember to pray for the five major world non-Christian religions: Tribal (usually animist beliefs), Hindu, Unreligious, Muslim and Buddhist.

Other important things to pray for here include: people involved with cults and other minor religions that exist throughout the world, nominal Christians, new and developing churches and ministries, government leaders in all levels of leadership, political situations and stability, and protection and courage for those being persecuted and for their persecutors.

Spiritual Life of Missionaries. Pray for their relationship with God to be healthy, their spiritual disciplines to remain in place, their daily sanctification and in-filling of the Holy

Spirit, their spiritual growth and maturity, their victory over temptation and sin, and their moral purity to remain intact. Pray also that they will experience confidence and joy in ministry.

Physical and Emotional Life of Missionaries. Pray for their physical and emotional health, safety and protection from any kind of harm or disease. Pray also for God's daily provision—financial needs, food, sufficient housing, transportation, education, rest, and stamina for life in a different culture—possibly in isolation from other team members or people from their own country or similar culture.

Family Life of Missionaries. Pray for their marriages and parent-child and sibling relationships to be healthy. For those workers who are single, pray for them to not be burdened with loneliness, for the Lord to bring close friends and partners in ministry into their life, and for discretion with members of the opposite gender. Pray also for the families and loved ones of workers who are at home, especially for those families that are unsupportive.

Ministry Life of Missionaries. Pray for their ability to learn and master different languages that may be needed for clear communication, their ability to communicate, their ability to adapt to and live and minister in another culture, their ministry requirements, and their ability to effectively manage time. Pray also for ministry opportunities to present themselves, as well as various professional relationships that exist with other missionaries, national church workers, and people in their community. Furthermore, pray for them to have favor in the eyes of the government (especially as it concerns residence visas and building permits, whether the government officials and policies are friendly toward Christians or not) and the people they work with.

Additional Workers. Offering prayers for the Lord to raise up more workers for the harvest taking place around the world is also very important. Jesus implores us to regularly and repeatedly ask the King of Heaven to raise up more spiritual shepherds and ministry leaders, especially to work among those people who have never heard of Jesus (Matthew 9:38). Throughout the history of the Church and of missions, this has been done, and the Lord has responded in some incredible ways when His people have prayed. When the Moravians gathered together to pray for world evangelism with 100 years of uninterrupted prayer, a great number of missionaries were sent throughout the 1700s. When a few students gathered together under a haystack in Massachusetts to pray for missions awareness among other college students, the foreign missionary movement of the 1800s began. When young people decided to commit to praying for missions and God's guidance regarding their involvement in missions, the Student Volunteer Movement sent out half of the American missionaries around the world in the early 1900s.[7] The lesson to be learned from history (and Scripture) is that God answers prayer. Therefore, the Church should be praying for a new generation of people to be recruited into missionary service.

Let Us Then Pray. Prayer is both the least we can do and the most we can do, no matter what size our church is. It is the least we can do because it is something we all can and should be practicing. All it takes for us to pray is our time and commitment to do it; no money is required. It is the most we can do because it is essential to what we do as we minister to people in this world. Prayer should undergird everything as we serve in mission together. Prayer is the first work, not the afterthought. May we then "become intercessors with a world vision that prays Satan-defeating, Kingdom-taking, people-reaching, captive-releasing, revival-giving, Christ-glorifying prayers!"[8]

Principle in Practice

Prayer is Primary

Cornerstone Church is a large Assemblies of God church in the city of Bowie, Maryland, that supports and partners with over 200 missionaries around the world while also thriving as a multicultural congregation that comprises of people from 55 different nations. As such, they are a strong missions-oriented church where every ministry program, including children's ministry, has an element of missions included within it.

Longtime pastor Mark Lehmann is very intentional about keeping this focus and has helped the church establish a "Strategy for World Ministries" to help everyone realize how foundational missions is to Cornerstone's existence. Of the seven principles laid out in this strategy, the very first one is seen as the most vital—prayer. For Cornerstone, "prayer is, and must continue to be, the primary gift we give to missions. Prayer connects the hearts of people within the local church to the heart of God and His love for the world. We understand that nothing of eternal value happens without prayer." These are not just words on paper, this is belief and conviction put into practice throughout each week of the year. This is what Pastor Lehmann also intimated to me in conversation.

Amid the flags of the nations represented in the congregation and the pictures of supported missionaries, both on display in the sanctuary, 50 to 500 people of all ages gather weekly on Saturday nights, even on holidays, for prayer. A significant part of the prayers is focused on missions and missionaries as hands are laid on each picture in a symbolic gesture of connection and blessing. Four times each year, this prayer time is led by a variety of diverse groups in the church, a sure way of involving as many people as possible in praying and prayer leadership. So strong is this emphasis on prayer that there are also teams of people who regularly gather throughout the week to keep connected with the missionaries, getting updates from them and encouraging them, then bringing their needs to the Lord in prayer together. The best thing about this, Lehmann says, is that "a church of *any size* can do it. It is free or low cost, and it has, perhaps, the most significant impact."

Suggested Resources

Jason Mandryk. *Operation World: The Definitive Prayer Guide to Every Nation* (7th ed.). Colorado Springs: Biblica, 2010.

Jason Mandryk. *Pray for the World: A New Prayer Resource from Operation World*. Downers Grove: InterVarsity Press, 2015.

Molly Wall and Jason Mandryk, eds. *Window on the World: An Operation World Prayer Resource*. rev. ed. Downers Grove: InterVarsity Press, 2018. (kid's version of *Operation World*)

Kids Praying for Kids DVD (resource for encouraging and teaching children to be intercessors for missions; available at http://www.prayershop.org/Kids-Praying-for-Kids-DVD-p/chi-rei-dv-001.htm) Websites: www.globalprayerdigest.org, joshuaproject.net/pray, www.operationworld.org

Notes

[1] J.D. Payne, *Strangers Next Door: Immigration, Migration and Mission* (Downers Grove: InterVarsity Press, 2012), 140.

[2] Jason Mandryk, *Operation World (7th ed.)* (Colorado Springs: Biblica, 2010), xxii.

[3] ACMC was founded in 1975 as a catalyst for missions mobilization in the local congregation, providing resources and training for a vast network of missions-minded churches. In 2007 it became part of the ministry of another missions organization known as Pioneers and was later dissolved in 2011.

[4] The full message, in written and audio format, can be accessed at http://www.desiringgod.org/resource-library/conference-messages/prayer-the-work-of-missions.

[5] Paul Borthwick, *How to Be a World-Class Christian* (Wheaton: Victor Books, 1991), 72-74.

[6] When posting prayer requests on the Internet, we need to be sure that they can be safely published in public, making sure that information about, or requests from, those serving in difficult places where persecution of Christians is occurring is not posted.

[7] See Kenneth Scott Latourette, *A History of Christianity: Beginnings to 1500*, rev. (San Francisco: Harper San Francisco, 1975) and *A History of Christianity: Reformation to the Present*, rev. (San Francisco: Harper San Francisco, 1975; Stephen Neill, *A History of Christian Missions*, rev. (New York: Penguin Books, 1986); Ruth A. Tucker, *From Jerusalem to Irian Jaya: A Biographical History of Christian Missions*, 2nd ed. (Grand Rapids: Zondervan, 2004).

[8] Jason Mandryk, *Pray for the World* (InterVarsity Press, 2015), xiii.

CHAPTER 5

GIVING TO MISSIONS

"The opportunities for using our financial resources to spread the gospel and strengthen the church all over the world are greater than they've ever been...The question is, what are we doing with that money? Our job is to make sure it gets to [God's] intended recipients."[1]

- Randy Alcorn -

"We are God's stewards of God's resources engaged in God's mission from everywhere to everywhere."[2]

- Sas Conradie -

Growing up, my parents always taught my brother and I about the importance of properly taking care of our money and possessions, which was consistently reinforced in the churches that we attended. Among other things, this meant that we were encouraged, when we earned any money, to give the first ten percent of whatever we earned to the church, and therefore to God. We were further encouraged to consider giving a little bit more to the work of missions, so that God's work around the world could be properly funded. From the very beginning, though I didn't know it then, we were instilled with the idea of being good stewards of what we have and how important it is to invest in God's work in this world. It is a practice that continues today, and something that my wife and I have tried to impart to our children.

Expanding on this a bit, we realize that taking part in God's mission is exciting work that is both a privilege and a responsibility that we have. Living this way, it is important for us to have a heart and vision for reaching the world for Christ. It is equally important to fund that vision to see that it gets accomplished. God is in control, and His purposes are always accomplished, but He still uses us in partnership with Him to see that the world is told about the good news of salvation and the arrival of God's kingdom in the person of Jesus. This is part of what I learned about money as I was growing up.

Throughout scripture we are invited to trust God and expected to take care of the resources He has given us, which includes wisely investing our finances in His kingdom operations. A basic understanding of financial stewardship, then, is a helpful starting point here as we consider what is involved with giving to missions.

Basic Stewardship. Before reading any further, take a moment to look up the following passages of scripture. The temptation here will be to merely note the references and move on. Resist that temptation and really read them to get a panoramic view of what God has to say about money, wealth, and stewardship. The passages are: Proverbs 3:9-10, 11:28, 13:7-8 & 11, 23:4-5, 22:7 & 16, 28:8 & 20-22, Matthew 6:19-34, Luke 16:1-13, 2 Corinthians 8:1-9, and 1 Timothy 6:3-10.

What follows is a summary of what is taught in these scripture passages, what can be called principles of financial stewardship.

Honor God with Our Money and Wealth. As God's people, we are expected to show our love for God entirely—heart, soul, mind, strength—in every area of our lives, putting Him first in everything, including all our resources (financial and otherwise). This happens when we give thanks to God for blessing us and when we practice trusting Him to continue to do so. This happens when we faithfully take care of and wisely use our money and other resources. This happens when we generously invest in *His* work and in the things related to *His* kingdom.

Keep God and His Kingdom the Top Priority. Recognizing how powerful money is, we are instructed in the scriptures to trust and pursue God rather than our accumulated wealth and personal gain. In fact, we are told repeatedly that we cannot love both God and money—that we can only serve or be friends with one of them, not both. Here is where it's important for us to look at our checkbooks, bank statements, and credit card bills to see where our allegiances appear to be, for therein lies our priorities. As Christ-followers, our heart attitude and motivations, along with our actions, should reflect a deep love for God, as well as a firm commitment to God's eternal kingdom and its concerns above all else rather than the things of this world that are temporary in the end. Among other things, this involves pursuing godliness with contentment as we trust God to provide for us what is needed in this life. In the ongoing battle of eternal treasure versus earthly wealth, that which is eternal must win.

Begin with the Tithe. When expressing love for God with our money, how much money should be set aside and invested in the work of God's Kingdom in this world? The answer to this question often depends on which books you are reading and which preachers and teachers you are listening to. In other words, there is more than one way to answer this question. Over the years, I have always taught that people should start with the literal tithe that we see described in the Scriptures, which is ten percent of every paycheck, and then increase the amount from there as the Lord blesses with more financial resources.[3] The tithe is a good guiding principle, but it is really only a start, as the scriptures encourage us to go further. The important thing to remember here is to give back to God a little bit of what is already His to begin with (He does own everything, after all) and to write Him the first check, the first-fruits of our earnings, to the local church, before any others are written to pay bills. Consideration can and should also be given to go above and beyond tithing to the church by also giving money as an offering to the work of missions beyond the local church (or to other special projects).

Be Faithful and Generous. As we respond to God's grace in our lives, we start to become more generous people who voluntarily, regularly, faithfully, sacrificially, and cheerfully give of our wealth and provisions. This generosity begins and ends with God. His goodness becomes *our* goodness, which we defer and deflect back to Him. This means investing in people, places, and projects where God is at work and where God directs us to give.

These biblical principles of financial stewardship further indicate that each of us are stewards of God's resources that He has given us and entrusted to our care. Good stewards are faithful, wise, financially responsible people who effectively, even strategically, manage what God has given them, using those things for the sake of God's kingdom rather than for personal gain. All of this directly impacts the mission of God in this world.

Why Give to the Work of Missions? So why give to the work of missions? Isn't it enough to give to my local church and to my church's local mission efforts? There are two simple, yet deeply profound, answers to this important question.

The first answer is related to what was just discussed. As stewards of God's resources, we are expected to regularly, generously, cheerfully, and sacrificially invest God's kingdom work in every part of the world, not just in our own parts of it.

The second answer is tied to the Great Commission that we have been given. God's mission is global in nature, and He has instructed us to engage in the mission locally *and* regionally *and* globally. Living in obedience to Jesus' instructions includes funding the work here, there, and everywhere. As local churches, we get to be financial partners in ministry with what God is doing around the world as we support the people, projects, and churches through which God is working.

The people in our churches should therefore be guided, encouraged, motivated, and challenged to be good stewards of their money and to discover what they can offer to the Church, the community, the nation, and the world. As such, it would be good for us to inspire acts of generosity within our churches and link financial acts of giving with acts of service by providing opportunities to give and serve locally and cross-culturally.

What does this look like in terms of funding the work of missions in particular?

How to Encourage Giving to Missions

The following action areas will be helpful for you as a pastor, missions mobilization team, or church board to prayerfully consider as you think about how to give to missions and how to encourage other people, of each generation, to give.

Communicate. There are three parties with whom we need to be in regular communication with. The first is God. When we are trying to decide who, where, and how much to give, it is imperative that we pray about it before we give, when we give, and after we give. This is an act of trust where we ask God to help us steward His money the best way that we can, even as we ask Him to further bless and multiply what is given for the sake of His kingdom.

The second party is the people in our congregation. This means that we should develop a culture of generosity where we teach, inspire, and invite people of all ages to be faithful and generous stewards who voluntarily and even sacrificially give to and invest in the work of missions around the world (ideally through the local church).[4] Be creative in how this is done, and help people to consider giving not just cash, but also items, property, or other assets that can be sold to generate even more money to be given away.[5] Along the way, we should also transparently report to our people updates about their investments, financial needs of missionaries and opportunities for giving, giving goals, and guidelines about how and where to give. Doing this will strengthen the interest and commitment levels of people as they develop a better awareness of where their money is going and deeper sense of relationship with those to whom they are giving.

The third party to keep communicating with is the missionaries themselves. As we support these cross-cultural workers, it is important that we make sure that they are invited and given freedom to openly communicate their financial needs at any point in the relationship. They should also be made aware of whatever the church's guidelines are as it relates to financially supporting missionaries. Depending on the relationship, it may also be helpful to keep missionary partners updated about how the church has met giving goals as it relates to missions or specific relevant missionaries.

Educate. Closely related to the need for communication is educating the people of our congregations as they grow as disciples of Jesus. In other words, we ought to be intentionally teaching them not just about *how* to give, but even more so about missions, kingdom stewardship, and eternal investments in our preaching, Sunday school classes, Bible study groups, one-on-one discussions and mentoring relationships, and other venues of instruction.[6]

By the way, starting to teach these points to people at a young age will not only help the younger generations understand stewardship earlier, but will also help the cause. Consider this: In December 2016, the Center for Parent/Youth Understanding reported that there were 25.6 million teenagers living in the United States at the time—teenagers with a national total annual income of $91.1 billion, with $208.7 billion spent on purchases for or by teens.[7] That means that if all these teenagers tithed, then around $9 billion could be given to the work of the church in one year. Even if only 25% of the teenaged population tithed, that would still bring in just over $2 billion. Living in the midst of Western wealth and materialism, with disposable income to spare, our Christian young people need to be encouraged to be good stewards of their resources and lives. In 1900, John R. Mott, the General Secretary for the World's Student Christian Federation in New York, captured the essence of this notion when he said that young people, "if *properly educated and guided*, are able to give and to raise each year a sum large enough to support all the foreign missionaries who would be required to accomplish the evangelization of the world."[8] What would happen if we invested in our young people in this way, teaching such things in our various outlets of ministry to children, teenagers, and college students?

Contemplate. Part of enhancing this process of giving will involve being aware of the needs of missionaries and missions efforts, world events, and how to best respond.

Also needed is some level of investigation and wise, strategic thinking through some of the "nuts and bolts" of your church's missions giving process. Here are some things to consider:

- Use discretion regarding who and what your church will support; if you are part of a denomination, I suggest giving to your denominational efforts first, especially those missionaries and projects that in some way have a personal connection to your church; if you are not part of denomination, or if you are giving to other organizations outside of your denomination, identify missionaries, projects, and organizations that align with your church's vision and strategy, as well as with those whom you have a relationship already established.

- Determine which initiatives and people are most strategic and what can best help; invest in long-term work over short-term pursuits.

- Consider focusing energy and financial resources on reaching the unreached and least-reached peoples of the world.

- Steer clear of creating relationships of dependency and giving to people, ministries, and projects that end up hurting people more than helping them[9].

- Decide how the process of giving to missions will function. Weigh out the benefits and drawbacks of such methods as creating a missions category in the church budget, faith promise giving, designated giving, special offerings, estate planning, or some combination of these things; be innovative and create other or new ways of giving.
- Avoid funding short-term missions trips from the church out of the church budget (or whatever method of missions funding you use), so that focus can properly be maintained on longer-term ministry efforts of the church or missions ministry; long-term investment trumps short-term bursts of activity, which can always be funded as individual projects.
- Decide how much you want to give to missions as a church and set realistic goals regarding how to reach that amount. Don't be afraid to raise the bar each year (or at least as-you-go); work hard to be more and more outward focused, even if by slow, incremental change[10].
- Bathe the whole process in prayer.

Celebrate. It is good for us to give thanks to God for how He is blessing us and providing for the people in our churches to give in this way. As we do this, we can build the momentum of being generous by celebrating mile markers and goals that we reach, noting how we continue to grow and how our kingdom investments are being used. We can do this in a variety of ways, all of which are public in nature (when appropriate and safe for our missionaries): notes in the worship service bulletin, announcements, ministry reports, church and ministry newsletters, church website, someone verbally sharing notes of "thanks for your support" from missionaries during worship services, and videos that report what's happening or

extend thanks from missionaries. Again, be creative in trying
to figure out other ways to do this—as long as you celebrate
what God is doing in you and through you in this world!

Relate. Relationships are key to this process. Indeed, it is
our tendency as human beings to give more to *people*, as opposed to projects, even when we don't even realize it or in-
tend to do it. So, we need to communicate with one another
and build relationships along the way. This includes pastors
and other church staff members being friends with those who
are part of the congregation. This involves the congregation
being intentional about truly caring for missionaries like they
are family, especially with those who were sent from or are
affiliated in some way with the church. And this also means
better connecting with people and churches with whom our
missionaries are working or with whom we may be ministry
partners. The stronger these relationships, the more likely our
investments in them will grow.

Collaborate. God has designed us to be together and to
work together, and the sooner we realize that the job of missions is too big to do by ourselves, the better. This includes the
giving aspect of missions, which means that it would be beneficial for us to work together with other churches, missions
organizations, and Christian philanthropy initiatives to fund
God's work around the world, work that is strategic, holistic,
and culturally sensitive as it truly impacts all areas of culture
and levels of society.

Demonstrate. Those of us who are leaders in our churches
should simply lead by example. People don't need to know
how much we give, but it is good for them know, through
some appropriate means, that we do give. When we lead in
this way, it adds to the credibility of the investment that we
are asking the people to make, making it much more likely
that they also will give. If you are a church leader, please lead

in this way; if you are not in that position, please encourage your leadership to lead accordingly.

Blessed to Give

As we encounter the principle in scripture that God blesses us so that we can then bless others, and that it is better for us to give than receive, it would be good for us to remember this in light of the worldwide work of God. We have an incredible opportunity to partner financially with what God is doing around the world! May we not lose sight of that, and may we fully invest ourselves in funding this work, encouraging others to join us in this grand venture.

Principle in Practice

Intentional Giving by Faith

Along the shoreline of Connecticut lies the town of Fairfield, home of a large non-denominational multisite church known as Black Rock Church. This historic church is well-known to many through its devotion to the work of mission throughout their community and around the world. Because it is seen as "integral to what is done at the church," according to missions pastor Larry Fullerton, one of the key strengths in this devotion is seen in their significant financial support of over sixty missionaries through faith promise giving, which amounts to roughly 23% of their annual budget. Some of these missionaries are "homegrown," while others are connected to the church different ways, but all of them serve with an established missions agency and all of them are financially supported by Black Rock in some way–up to 50% of their support in many cases.

To help encourage this investment and support, Black Rock does a number of things throughout the year, including a large missions festival to support local mission efforts, a large missions conference to support global mission work (the 3rd largest event of the year), and monthly updates in the worship gatherings that help to show how the church is having an impact on the lives and ministries of their supported missionaries. So important is this focus, that the church even builds it into their membership classes, making it a part of the congregational DNA. Along the way, Pastor Fullerton indicates, "70% of the congregation has bought in, giving generously to the work of the Great Commission around the world. The key is to challenge people to make contributions and then help them see how those contributions make a difference in the world."

Personalized Giving

Cornerstone Christian Fellowship is a small Assemblies of God congregation in the suburban community of Fountain Valley in Orange County, California. When Karl Vaters became the pastor here in 1992, the church was broken in nearly all areas of ministry. They were inward-focused and needed to be healed. The good news is that twenty-six years later, a once unhealthy church is "now healthy but moving toward becoming healthful" (their story is shared by Vaters in his book, *The Grasshopper Myth: Big Churches, Small Churches and the Small Thinking that Divides Us*).

As part of this movement forward, a new outlook on missions arose after Pastor Vaters returned from a ministry experience at an orphanage in Bucharest, Romania, as his newfound passion spread among the people of the congregation. As a result, teams from the church began to serve at the orphanage, a ministry partnership was formed, and the spark of mission involvement quickly became a flame that continues to burn today. One of the stronger pieces of Cornerstone's missions involvement is their giving to the work of the mission. With great intent, their focus of giving is entirely based on relationships. "Relational connections," Vaters says, "are the heart of the church. We put a lot of hard work into developing relationships with one another and with the missionaries that we support."

With this in mind, they financially support only those missionaries who have been sent from their church and missionaries or projects that they have personally visited or about which they are especially impassioned. This streamlined approach keeps the relational ties stronger and more personal. This also helps them be better, more intentional, stewards of the financial resources they have at their disposal.

Suggested Resources

Randy Alcorn. *Money, Possessions, and Eternity*. rev. ed. Wheaton: Tyndale House Publishers, Inc., 2003.

Randy Alcorn. *The Treasure Principle: Unlocking the Secret of Joyful Giving*. rev. ed. Colorado Springs: Multnomah, 2017.

Craig L. Blomberg. *Christians in an Age of Wealth: A Biblical Theology of Stewardship*. Grand Rapids: Zondervan, 2013.

Jonathan J. Bonk. *Missions and Money: Affluence as a Western Missionary Problem*. Maryknoll: Orbis Books, 1991.

Michael Rhodes, Robby Holt, and Brian Fikkert. *Practicing the King's Economy: Honoring Jesus in How We Work, Earn, Spend, Save, and Give*. Grand Rapids: Baker Books, 2018.

Notes

[1] Randy Alcorn, *Money, Possessions, and Eternity*, rev. ed. (Wheaton: Tyndale House Publishers, Inc., 2003), 239.

[2] Sas Conradie, "Global Stewardship in the 21st Century," in *Kingdom Stewardship: Occasional Papers Presented by the Lausanne Resource Mobilization Working Group for Cape Town 2010*, ed. Arif Mohamed, Brett Elder, and Stephen Grabill (Grand Rapids: Christian's Library Press, 2010), 49.

[3] For many people, this percentage puts a real strain on the household budget. To them I say to make it a matter of prayer—to make this decision with the Lord—regarding what percentage to begin working with and building from. Whether this is off the net amount or the gross amount of pay is also debated; I suggest the gross pay, but again encourage making this a matter of prayer.

[4] Consider Craig Blomberg's insight here, "Believers have the resources to alleviate enormous amounts of human suffering apart from relying either on the secular business world or the government. If the church had the will to do so, it could make a huge difference and make it clear to the world that its ministry was in Jesus' name. Imagine how many more people would become Christ's followers as a result!" (Craig L. Blomberg, *Christians in an Age of Wealth* (Grand Rapids: Zondervan, 2013), 26-27.

[5] A great example of this happened at the LIFE 2007 event conducted by The Christian & Missionary Alliance for high school students. At this five-day conference, one of the things that the attenders were challenged with was tangibly connecting to the work of The C&MA in Africa through Project 132 (1 continent to expose, 3 hours to entertain, 2 ways to engage). This culminated with a missions-themed worship service near the end of the conference, which included the collection of an offering for this work. As reported in a denominational press release at the time, "A total of $117,280 was collected in a cash offering for Project 132. Many of the teens were moved to give their own personal belongings—watches, jewelry, iPods, a Nintendo Game Boy, a compact disc player, a camera, and a camcorder. Stu-

dents also donated first-aid equipment, clothing, linens, hygiene
items, eyeglasses, school supplies, French Bibles, New Testaments,
and more to fill a 40-foot shipping container that is being sent
to Burkina Faso, West Africa." (The Christian & Missionary Alliance. *LIFE 2007: American Teens Respond to Africa's Challenges*, July
25, 2007. http://www.cmalliance.org/news/2007/07/25/life-2007-
american-teens-respond-to-africas-challenges/)

[6]Mark Sigmon, of Global Impact Services, says it well, "People will
put their money where their heart is: when you speak often of God's
passion and your bold ministry vision, they will respond. The key?
Explain the right motives...and utilize the best methods." (Mark Sigmon, *Global Impact Manual: The Essential Roadmap for Your Mission
to the Nations* (Jenison, MI: Global Impact Services, 2009), 48.

[7]Walt Mueller, "Kids, Christmas, and Too Much Stuff...", *Learning My
Lines*, December 14, 2016, http://cpyu.org/2016/12/14/kids-christ-
mas-and-too-much-stuff/.

[8]Quoted in Edwin M. Bliss et al., eds., *Ecumenical Missionary Conference, New York, 1900: Report of the Ecumenical Conference on Foreign
Missions, Held in Carnegie Hall and Neighboring Churches, April 21 to
May 1*, vol. 1 (New York: American Tract Society, 1900), 99. (emphasis added)

[9]I highly recommend the following resources: Steve Corbett and
Brian Fikkert, *When Helping Hurts: How to Alleviate Poverty Without
Hurting the Poor—and Yourself*, rev. ed. (Chicago: Moody Publish-
ers, 2012) and Robert D. Lupton, *Toxic Charity: How Churches and
Charities Hurt Those They Help (And How to Reverse It)* (New York:
HarperCollins Publishers, 2011).

[10]How much of our church income should be going to the mission?
In a missions class taken at Gordon-Conwell Theological Seminary,
my mentor, Dr. Peter Kuzmic, once suggested that churches should
be giving 75-80% of their annual budget to outward-focused activities (local, regional, and global). I agree with him that the majority
of what is taken in and budgeted should reflect such a commitment,
however I have found it challenging to get churches to adopt this way
of thinking; it's certainly not impossible, though. Randy Alcorn said

it well, "There is no greater way to invest our money in eternity than in the cause of world missions. All of us should be giving regularly to our local churches, and we should encourage our leaders in turn to invest an even larger share of their church budgets in world missions," (Randy Alcorn, *Money, Possessions, and Eternity*, 240).

CHAPTER 6

SENDING AND CARING FOR MISSIONARIES

""We saw," said Fuller afterwards, "there was a gold mine [i.e. opportunities for ministry among the unreached] in India, but it was as deep as the center of the earth. Who will venture to explore it? 'I will venture to go down,' said [William] Carey, 'but remember that you...must hold the ropes.' We solemnly engaged to him to do so, nor while we live shall we desert him."[1]

- George Smith -

"The effectiveness of those who go is contingent on those who serve as senders.[2]

- Neal Pirolo -

In my high school and college years, people noticed my interest in missions develop into a passion and I suspect that many assumed that I would someday be a missionary living in another culture. I never rejected that possibility, but I also never felt compelled to pursue it. As I grew older, got married, and started a family, I remained involved with missions-related ventures and continued to learn and grow in my abilities to lead and mobilize others in this regard. All the while, I remained open to the possibility that the Lord could still ask my wife and I to be missionaries somewhere else in the world. In fact, we have twice explored this option, and I have pursued pastorates in international churches abroad. Every time, the Lord has let us know that He wants us exactly where He already has us, in the United States, mobilizing people to be missionally involved, participating globally via short-term ministry opportunities, and living life without regret as senders of missionaries rather than goers.

As we live in a way where we are committed to missions and to what God is doing around the world, we quickly understand, as I did, that some people are called to go to another culture to serve as missionaries, while others are called to stay in their own culture and serve God there. Both kinds of people are engaging in God's mission, both are valuable and strategic to God's work in this world, both are needed to accomplish the task.

When someone is sent on a mission (in this case, those we refer to as missionaries), then someone should send them. Once they go, the senders should stay invested in their lives and care for them. Missionaries may be heroic to some degree, but they are not invincible superheroes who stand alone to do the work. Remember, we are on mission *together*. So how does this work? What is involved with sending missionaries and caring for them?

Senders Needed

First things first. As mentioned, senders are needed. As the apostle Paul reminds us in Romans 10:13-15, "'Everyone who calls on the name of the Lord will be saved.' How, then, can they call on the one they have not believed in? And how can they believe in the one of whom they have not heard? And how can they hear without someone preaching to them? And how can anyone preach unless they are sent? As it is written:

'How beautiful are the feet of those who bring good news!'" What this tells us is that senders of missionaries are just as important as those who go as missionaries and the Church should always keep this dynamic of sending and going at the forefront of missional ministry.

What if a local church has never sent out a missionary? Are they failing to do their part in the global work of God? No, absolutely not! Even though a congregation may have never sent someone to do cross-cultural ministry long-term, it doesn't mean they should not participate in the process of sending by keeping the need for more international workers before the people. And even if no missionaries have been sent from a particular church, it doesn't prevent a church from partnering with other churches in the sending process. It certainly doesn't prevent a church from caring for those who have been sent. This activity of sending and caring, by the way, does not depend on the size of the congregation or its budget. I personally know of small churches that have sent missionaries from their midst or are active participants in caring for missionaries in various ways. I also know large churches that have done neither.

Sending and Caring

So then, how does a church of any size go about the process of sending missionaries and caring for them or caring for missionaries that are somehow connected to the church? What are some steps that your church can take? Here are some ways to respond as people who are called to send rather than go. Ideally, these responses would be under the leadership of the church's Missions Mobilization Team.

Prepare and Develop. The sending and caring process begins before missionaries are even sent as the church commits to their continued spiritual development and to preparing them for life on the mission field. As Carlton Vandagriff and Joel Sutton so aptly point out in the prologue to *Whom Shall We Send? Understanding the Essentials of Sending Missionaries:*

> *It's…not fair to prospective personnel to send them out merely based on their personal claim to be called and prepared. Churches and agencies owe these workers a discipleship process that helps them determine if they are mentally, emotionally, physically, and spiritually ready for the rigors and demands of cross-cultural life and ministry. This deep discipleship can help candidates confirm and clarify their calling as well as discover where that calling can best be fulfilled in the missions setting.[3]*

Good preparation and development will include assisting missionary candidates with understanding their passions, talents, strengths, spiritual gifts, and vocational calling, while also evaluating such things as their moral character, ministry faithfulness, knowledge of scripture and theology, and cross-cultural ministry preparedness. This process will also involve helping them meet appropriate educational requirements or professional development needs[4] that will contribute to their thriving both personally and vocationally on the mission field. It is also important here to help them find and get established with the right sending agency, which may be your denomination, or any number of missions agencies that exist, or even your church itself if you are able.

Pray. It has already been pointed out earlier how vital it is that we pray for missionaries, and I refer you back to Chapter Four for further insight into prayer as a way of loving and caring for cross-cultural ministry workers. When you take the time to really know them and embrace them as family members, praying for missionaries becomes more natural and effective as we ask the Lord to bless them in specific ways. One helpful way to keep missionary friends and family "near" to us is to keep their prayer cards and requests prominently displayed as reminders, both for us privately and at in our church facilities.

Communicate. Communication is essential for healthy relationships of all kinds and communicating with missionaries is no different. As much as we can, we should work hard to stay in touch with these family members and let them know they are not forgotten and that we are standing with them. Through writing letters, emailing, calling, connecting through various social media platforms, and even sending video letters we are able to stay in touch with one another as we share news, encourage and support one another, celebrate life together, cry together, and pray for one another. And along the way, we never fail to miss an opportunity to extend birthday love, anniversary congratulations, or holiday greetings.

Assist. A big part of caring for missionaries once they've been sent is found in assisting them in three key ways. The first of these is helping them financially by doing things like generously contributing to their housing, transportation, and general cost of living expenses while creatively making each dollar last for both sender and sent ones alike. Also helpful here is preparing them and encouraging them to manage their money well as good stewards of their resources.

The second way to assist missionaries is by helping to meet their practical, day-to-day living needs. This even includes helping them before they leave to collect, pack, and ship items to resettle with in their new home. Once on the field, missionaries may need some help with things like securing housing, transportation, schooling for kids, health care, and a variety of other things that the church and its members can provide. Simple things, like sending gifts and care packages on special occasions, can be a significant help. Gift cards for various online retailers are cheap and easy to send and allow the missionaries to get what they need or want.[5] We can also help by watching over items and property of missionaries while they are gone; in some cases, we may also assist with the care of family members.

Occasionally, missionaries will encounter times of crisis in their lives. Perhaps, for example, they are the only missionaries around and loneliness and severe depression have set in. Perhaps they have witnessed or somehow become innocently entangled in an international incident like a car bombing or other act of terrorism. Perhaps someone on their team has died.[6] In such times, we can step in and provide needed help. Sometimes, the crisis is personal in nature and we can offer counseling by ways of professional help through video chat or telephone. If needed or preferred, we can also pay for professional counseling to happen in person wherever they are (if such service is accessible) or we could even send a professional counselor to go to them in person. Sometimes the situation is much more traumatic in nature and professional help is clearly needed. Paying for or sending a trauma counselor to them is a way to show that we care. In extreme cases, we may need to help get them home in an emergency, whether from trauma experienced, medical or political evacuation, or even death (both in the field or at home)

Provide Pastoral Care. One final way to show our love and care for missionaries is to help provide them with pastoral care. Although they may attend church where they are serving, and though they may be part of a team of people who are ministering to one another, nothing beats receiving pastoral care from the missionary's own pastor and church. Many times, those in smaller churches (and medium-sized churches) feel that they are not able to do this due to budgetary restraints. The truth, however, is that any sized church can accomplish this with little-to-no financial investment. How? Simply by staying in touch with the missionaries connected to the church through such things as writing letters, sending emails, making phone calls, or contacting them through Skype or some other kind of video chat just to encourage, lend an ear, provide basic counseling, and pray for and with those who have been sent.

It's also good to visit missionaries in person where they are serving in ministry, when possible. I would suggest that each missionary family that is connected to a church ought to be visited by the pastor of that church at least once per term being served. If the church is smaller, then the pastor can try to make a visit at least once in his/her tenure as pastor. If a church has more than one pastor on staff, such visits should not fall exclusively to the missions pastor; rather, all the pastors, especially the senior pastor, should be involved with this. Even better would be teams of people, led by a pastor, who would go and serve the missionaries in this capacity. Churches of all sizes should commit to making this a priority and should work to make it financially possible. After all, those who were sent are part of the congregation that sent them and they, too, need a pastor.

Re-Entry Support and Care

The care for our sent ones is not just for getting them there and helping them while they are on the field, it is also for when they are back home for their home assignment ministry and fund-raising tours, as well as for other reasons such as retirement or a family emergency. At this point, we should care for them in the same ways we do when they are away, but we need to remember that things are different for them again as they settle back to life in their home culture. When missionaries come home, as Neal Pirolo points out, they are often not sure about how they fit in their community–socially, materially, or spiritually.[7] So what can we do? In addition to continuing the things mentioned in the previous section, here are some suggestions for what local churches, in partnership with any sending agencies that may be involved, can do.

Help Them Readjust. As mentioned, things have likely changed, sometimes dramatically, in the home culture and a period of readjustment is often needed. Most denominations and other sending agencies have conferences for their international workers to attend that will help here, but local churches can go even further and hopefully be even more personal. We can help here by doing simple things for missionaries like taking them shopping for clothes that are now in style or helping them get acquainted with the latest technology. Coming alongside them in this way helps the process go a lot quicker, or at least a lot smoother. This is especially important for missionary kids, who are kids just like ours who are just trying to fit-in to another culture as a Third-Culture Kid.[8]

Practice Hospitality. When missionaries return home, they still have basic needs that must be met, like housing, transportation, and salary. We can help them out here by simply continuing to serve them during their experience at home. Such hospitality begins at the airport. If they don't have family that can meet them there, then this becomes a great opportunity for members from their church family to meet them and get them to where they will be staying, whether temporarily or for their whole home assignment, which may even be provided by the church or someone in the church. A bonus blessing here would be to have the kitchen fully stocked and the place fully furnished so that they have one less thing to worry about as they resettle. Setting them up with a vehicle to use is also helpful, as is connecting them with people from the church or community who can help them with free or low-cost care for such things as medical and dental needs, car needs, legal needs, and financial service. We also want to connect with them personally during their time at home by having them over for meals, taking them out to eat on occasion, and involving them in other social activities. In terms of a paycheck, any financial support that is given to them when they are on the field should be continued when they return home as well.

Provide Pastoral and Professional Care. When our missionaries are home, this is a chance to minister pastorally to them in more personal ways. Pastoral care should obviously continue as we provide them various kinds of opportunities to recharge physically, mentally, and spiritually. For the times they are around, help them get plugged in with church activities beyond the Sunday worship service, make the kids feel welcome in the children's and youth ministries, invite them to be part of a small group, even send them on a weekend retreat somewhere to help them get revitalized. It is also possible, depending on the circumstances surrounding their reason for being home, that our international workers could use some professional counseling help. In such times, we can help make that happen.

Allow Them to Minister. One other important thing to remember is that our sent ones have a story to share. As important as it is for us to serve them, we should also let them serve us and minister to and with us. Allow them to share their story with us in as many venues as we can, among all the age groups in the church, such as worship services, church school classes, small groups, and so on. It would also be good to encourage and help them to share their story with other churches and groups, too, especially if there are other people, churches, or organizations that also serve as financial or prayer supporters.

Relational Connections (Hold the Ropes)

In the end, caring for those we send out as missionaries comes down to relationship. Indeed, the essence of being on mission *together* is being in relationship with one another and we must do whatever it takes to make sure this happens in a healthy, mutually supportive way. Like William Carey's friends held the "ropes" for him as he served in India in the late 18th and early 19th centuries, so we stand with our brothers and sisters whom we send, supporting them in the same way, knowing that our role as senders is just as important as being sent. As senders, then, we get to know our missionaries and their ministries, and we commit to actively collaborating with them in their endeavors for Christ. Together, in relationship, we do the work that the Lord has laid before us to make worshipers of the living God and followers of Jesus Christ among all peoples in this world. May it be so in each of our churches as we partner together in the *missio Dei.*

Principle in Practice

It's Not Just the Money

Grace Bible Church is a 53-year-old multisite Independent Bible Church in College Station, Texas, near Texas A&M University. One of their foundational values is missions, which Grace's missionary care pastor Pat Coyle describes in part, as "giving liberally out of a relatively meager church budget in order to send, support, and encourage those who go as missionaries, particularly to the unreached and least reached peoples in this world." Grace currently supports in some way around 100 full-time workers locally, regionally, and globally, most of whom consider Grace Bible Church their home church as they were mobilized and sent from here. How does Grace help care for these workers?

It's seen in the relationships that are established, which makes their commitment to them more personal and much easier to do as it comes out of genuine love for one another. So important are these relationships, and so strong is this love, Coyle says, that "unless there is a doctrinal or other serious reason, [they] do not sever existing relationships—[they] consider the support relationship a long-term commitment between the church and those who [they] send." As such, financial support is provided through monthly giving as well as occasional one-time gifts for projects or personal needs. But it's not just about the money, it's also about the prayer and ongoing moral and emotional support, as seen in how various small groups within the church adopt missionaries for such care, even blessing them financially and in other practical ways, like with annual Christmas gifts.

Additionally, the church's missions staff and other church leaders make it a point to try to visit missionaries on the field every three to five years to keep building the friendships and provide encouragement and more personalized pastoral care. When missionaries are on home assignment and reside in the area, the church also has two homes available for their use at a very low cost. Members of Grace's Missionary Care Team have received training to help missionaries with basic debriefing and counseling needs, as well as any needed professional care, when they are home.

Pastor Coyle also offers the following advice to any size church. "First, start with what seems reasonably doable as a step of faith, but start! Intention to lavishly support missions/missionaries doesn't happen 'once you're ready'. Second, challenge your own to go. And get behind them, even if initially for just a little while. Let them know that you are standing with them. Third, make your budgetary commitment to missions up front—choose by faith, put it in a budget, and plan to spend it. If our commitment from the beginning hadn't been 'up front, we are going to invest in blessing the nations,' this would never have been achieved in our resource-restrained environment."

They're Family

In 2007, Pastor Jonathan Matias led an effort to plant a church inside the most densely populated section of the beltway of Washington, D.C., in the city of Alexandria, Virginia. From the very beginning, this small non-denominational church known as Grace Church of Alexandria was multiculturally-minded and specifically ministered to the Ethiopian community that exists there. This soon expanded to include people from Afghanistan and various parts of Asia, who are also among the ninety countries of origin and 120 language groups that exist in the Alexandria Community.

Grace Church was not content just ministering to those in their community, they also sent or significantly assisted several missionaries over the years and have made it an intentional practice to care for those they sent or are partnered with in ministry. For this church, it's "all about the relationship" and "loving them well in the context of relationship, because love is the linchpin," according to Matias. In fact, supported missionaries are embraced as family by the people at Grace Church. Indeed, the question that is drilled deep into the psyche of this congregation is, "What kind of care would you want to receive if you were far away from your family?"

So, this aspect of caring is obviously extremely important for them. How does this happen? One way is through Pastor Matias and other missions advocates making frequent contact with the workers through media variety of means. In these times, friendships are strengthened, needs are shared and taken care of, and people are prayed for. A second way that the relationships are made stronger is regular Skype or Google Hangout interviews and discussions with the congregation during weekly worship gatherings. A third way of caring that the church is committed to is seen in their ongoing prayer and financial support for their missionaries. Financially speaking, they simply share what they have, out of who they are, and try to help fund a significant percentage of what missionaries need, budgeting what they can out of the church's general fund.

In 2018, this church closed. The work they did for the Kingdom and the investments they made in the mission, however, did not die and the fruit of their labor has not disappeared. There is much to glean from their example.

Suggested Resources

Steve Beirn with George W. Murray. *Well Sent: Reimagining the Church's Missionary Sending Process*. Ft. Washington, PA: CLC Publications, 2015.

Glenn Hanna. *Building Missionaries: Fostering Souls for Success on the Field*. Pittsburgh: Urban Press, 2018.

Neal Pirolo. *Serving As Senders Today*. rev. & exp. San Diego: Emmaus Road International, Inc., 2012.

Neal Pirolo. *The Reentry Team: Caring for Your Returning Missionaries*. San Diego: Emmaus Road International, 2000.

Joel Sutton, ed. *Whom Shall We Send?: Understanding the Essentials of Sending Missionaries*. Self-Published, CreateSpace, 2016.

Trinity Church Missionary Care Team. *Mind the Gaps: Engaging the Church in Missionary Care*. Kansas City, MO: Mind the Gaps, 2015.

Notes

[1] George Smith, C.I.E., LL.D., *The Life of William Carey: Shoemaker & Missionary*, rep. (New York: E.P. Dutton & Co., 1913), 41. Another biography of Carey relates it this way, "The [Particular Baptist Society for the Propagation of the Gospel Amongst the Heathen] could hardly pause for shrewd debate about ways and means. The fountains of the deep were opened, and they hasted to commit themselves in faith to the support of the two." (S. Pearce Carey, *William Carey* (London: The Wakeman Trust, 1923), 96.

[2] Neal Pirolo, *Serving As Senders Today*, rev. & exp. (San Diego: Emmaus Road International, Inc., 2012), 5.

[3] Joel Sutton, ed., *Whom Shall We Send?* (Self-Published, CreateSpace, 2016), 5.

[4] Caleb Crider suggests that churches minimally focus "efforts toward the development of these characteristics: sound doctrine, good stewardship, and devotion to a missional lifestyle" as they develop ministry workers and potential missionaries. (Sutton, *Whom Shall We Send?*, 225)

[5] It is worth taking a little bit of time here to find out from the missionaries what online retailers they have access to in the country where they serve.

[6] I personally know several missionaries who have experienced these very things.

[7] Neal Pirolo, *The Reentry Team* (San Diego: Emmaus Road International, 2000), 16.

[8] "A Third Culture Kid (TCK) is a person who has spent a significant part of his or her developmental years outside the parents' culture. The TCK frequently builds relationships to all of the cultures, while not having full ownership in any. Although elements from each culture may be assimilated in the TCK's life experience, the sense of belonging is in relationship to others of similar background." (David Pollock, quoted in David C. Pollock and Ruth E. Van Reken, *Third Culture Kids*, rev. ed. (Boston: Nicholas Brealey Publishing, 2009), 13.

CHAPTER 7

MISSIONS EXPOSURE AND MINISTRY EXPERIENCES

"If we are going to accomplish the global purpose of God, it will not be primarily through giving our money, as important as that is. It will happen through giving ourselves. This is what the gospel represents, and it's what the gospel requires."[1]

- David Platt -

"It is inexcusable for Christians in the US to not engage in cross-cultural evangelization for it can be done at home in ethnic conclaves domestically."[2]

- Enoch Wan -

By now you have likely discerned that I love to be around people from other cultures, whether in my own community or in another part of the world. I also enjoy serving people in ministry in a variety of capacities. One blessing that comes from these passions is that I can participate in cross-cultural ministry, even though I have not been sent as a missionary, and so can you.

As people and churches that are involved with missions, our participation should move beyond giving to missions, praying for missions, and sending and caring for our missionaries. There is no reason why we can't also more fully and personally engage in the mission ourselves. What follows in this chapter, then, are three ways that we can do this, and each of them are not as intimidating as they may sound: cross-cultural ministry involvement, serving internationals in the community and region, and being a multicultural congregation.

Cross-Cultural Ministry Involvement

Following the lead of Jesus, a variety of ministry opportunities should be provided year-round in a manner that appeals to everyone's interests and skill levels while allowing them to serve the Lord and others that practically makes use of people's spiritual gifts, passions, talents, and abilities. Many people, especially among the younger generations, are civic-minded and concerned with causes of various kinds, strongly desiring to make a difference in the world by doing important work that helps others. As such, people in our churches, especially children, teens, and young adults, can be given the chance to be stewards of their time and talents by making opportunities available for them to make a difference through ministry in the local church and in the community and region in which they live.

For many, this will help them become more outward-focused and not so self-centered while they are challenged to love God and love others while living in obedience to the Great Commission. In fact, it is here, in local and regional missional living, that many folks sense God's leading to international or cross-cultural ministry as international workers somewhere else in the world.

Such local and regional ministry should then nudge us to go further, to places all over the world. Perhaps one of the more obvious ways to do this is by participating in short-term missions experiences, either as individuals with a short-term missions agency or as a team of people from a church or collection of churches.[3] An important part of long-term missions involvement at any level is positive shorter-term experiences in a cross-cultural context that allow for exposure to other cultures, to the mission field, and to missionaries, as well as provide some hands-on ministry experience in a cross-cultural situation. In these situations, participants are thrust out of their comfort zones and challenged to be outward-focused, perhaps to a greater degree than with local ministry involvement. The importance of such experiences cannot be overstated. Missions agencies and denominations have come to see them as extremely important and integral to the process of missions mobilization and recruitment of future missionaries. Paul Borthwick summarizes this widely held opinion particularly as it relates to the younger generations, noting that experiences "in missions service... are perhaps the most critical element needed in expanding the world view of young people. These experiences show students that... they can make a difference!"[4]

Let me be very clear, such experiences should not replace the long-term process of incarnational ministry by vocational missionaries! Rather, short-term projects should be part of long-term strategy. Such an approach prioritizes the goals and needs of the mission, the national church, and the missionaries in a long-term, holistic contextual strategy for evangelization and church planting. Short-term projects then become one way of achieving these goals and objectives, and field leadership helps determine the purpose of the short-term missions experiences. This is one way that senders and receivers can strive for partnership in the work of world evangelization.

To infuse such a cross-cultural dimension to the Great Commandment and the Great Commission into ministry programming, your church can offer two types of short-term missions related experiences, either independently as a church or working with their denomination's national office or other missions agency. The first type is a vision trip, where a group of people goes to a particular mission field not to do ministry per se, but to be inspired about God's global work and to observe and interact with missionaries and nationals, therefore developing a new or renewed vision for missions or for a particular part of the world; ministry still happens along the way. Such a trip could also be done with the intent of gathering information regarding the setting up of a ministry partnership between the church and the mission field.

The second type of short-term experience sets intentional cross-cultural ministry involvement as its goal. This could involve efforts such as work projects, running camps or Bible schools, street evangelism, drama or puppet ministry, music ministry, medical work, or even prayer walking; a vision for missions is further developed along the way. Of course, these experiences should be in alignment with the goals of the mission field and done in a way so as not to interfere with ministry or the work of the missionaries.[5]

As these types of experiences are planned, certain things should be kept in mind for them to be effective and done right.

1. Long-term field strategy must be kept in mind. Short-term missions experiences should not be used to replace long-term incarnational ministry. They should be incorporated into the designed to help the process along.

2. A participant's and church's motivation should be clear in regard to why they want to participate in a short-term project. A consumer mindset and selfish motives should to be avoided, as these are not for tourism or resume-building. Rather, these are ministry trips that are designed to help in the work of world evangelization. The fact that participants are blessed and grow spiritually during these experiences is just an added benefit. Short-term teams should therefore be carefully selected, with fewer people who have right intentions and who are motivated by the heart of a servant ready to minister. Teams should also be established based on field needs and an individual's ministry gifts and skills; people should be matched to appropriate types of ministry. Project, team, and field expectations should also be established and clarified prior to departure to the project location.

3. There should be adequate preparation and training for the experience; participants need to go prepared. This should include such things as country and culture orientation, basic language and cultural issues, culture shock concerns, criminal background check, medical insurance and release, and team-building activities. Many excellent training resources are available to help in this process.

4. Maximize the experience while on the mission field or project site by having ongoing field orientation, regular debriefing sessions, and frequent times of prayer as a team.

5. Conduct at least one follow-up session after returning home as a way of making sense of the experience and discussing how to apply the lessons of the experience to everyday life.

6. Follow-through with those participants, especially children or young adults, who become more committed to long-term missions involvement. Encourage these individuals and help them to develop a lasting global impact. This is especially important in the process of helping young adults discern God's leading for them to become vocational workers.

One way, then, that local churches can be on mission together is through cross-cultural ministry experiences. There are no age restrictions or limits on one's ability to be involved here, only a willingness to commit to the work and serve. Will there be challenges and setbacks? Yes, but the benefits fully outweigh them when the experiences are done right.

Consider also the tremendous value of going beyond short-term experiences to establishing long-term ministry partnerships where church groups, churches, or a grouping of churches, enter into a collaborative relationship of trust and commitment to help one another engage in God's mission and fulfil what God has compelled them to do. Such a partnership can happen with a specific missionary or missionary team, a specific project or cause, an individual or church in another country or culture, or within a country that is of special interest. If there are missionaries that have been sent from the church (or missionaries with whom the church has a special connection), these are already natural starting points for such a partnership to begin.[6] In this relationship, all partners pray for one another, help meet one another's needs, share resources, visit one another, and do ministry together, all while growing together as friends who are on mission together. When this kind of investment happens, missions becomes even more personalized and strategic.

Serving Internationals in the Community and Region

Another way we can engage in the mission is to recognize that people have come to us from other nations in the world. Indeed, we don't need to get on a plane or a boat to travel to the other side of the world, we can be involved in cross-cultural ministry in our own neighborhoods and throughout the region in which we live by simply serving internationals who live among us, namely migrants, immigrants, refugees,[7] and international students.

As I write this, we who live in the United States continue to argue and debate about how to respond to migrant workers, immigrants, and refugees.[8] This is not a book that is specifically focused on this topic, so I will not expand here on my political views except to share my opinion that the current system regarding immigrants and refugees in the United States is clearly broken and is in desperate need of reform that is both compassionate and wise.

It is helpful for us to first have a broad understanding of what the Bible says about such things so that we have a foundation to build from. The first thing we want to note here is the reminder that God is in control of all things, and sometimes He moves people around, often for them to either be in a better position to hear about Him and His message of love, hope, and grace. Sometimes, however, He moves people around to be the ones who share that message.[9] We also want to remember that we are mandated throughout the scriptures to love people as God does, not to simply tolerate them. This includes foreigners, refugees, and enemies.[10] Loving people involves practicing hospitality and extending mercy while also helping to meet people's needs, particularly those who are disenfranchised and vulnerable (like the materially poor, orphans, widows, immigrants, and refugees). Love also involves necessarily taking risks on people, without expecting anything in return. Of course, the prime example of such love is Jesus Christ (who is also identified as one of the vulnerable people in Matthew 25). One other thing to recall is that we are also instructed to obey the laws of man unless they contradict the law of God.[11]

Building from these reminders from scripture, what are some steps for us to take as individuals and churches? How can we effectively serve the internationals who live in our communities and throughout the region in which we live? Let me suggest five ways, which are outlined below.

Proactive Posture. Many times, when we are uncomfortable with, misunderstand, or just aren't paying attention to situations in life, we just react without necessarily giving it another thought. In the case of immigrants and refugees, it would be more helpful to respond with a more proactive stance where we prepare for what is likely to come rather than react to what is already a reality. With this kind of an approach, then, we can posture ourselves more effectively by putting together a plan to serve migrants and immigrants (whether documented or not), refugees, and international students for the sake of the gospel.

Prepare the Church. Being prepared for ministry to internationals includes thinking through and teaching: what the

Bible says about missions and missional living (locally, regionally, globally); how we are to treat immigrants, refugees, and other foreigners who live among us; and how we may be able to biblically respond to immigration reform and the refugee situation. Good preparation also includes discerning and developing a plan for how to invest in international students who attend nearby colleges and universities or who are being hosted as foreign exchange students in the local schools.[12] Two good questions to try to answer here are: "What is God already doing?" and "How can I be a part of that?"

Practice Hospitality. Essentially, this means that we should be generous hosts to all types of people from other cultures, no matter who they are, where they're from, or what their religion is. This sets the example for the rest of society. Some practical ways to practice such hospitality include: helping new international residents to get settled by helping them find housing while providing them basic items like food, clothing, and furniture, showing them where to shop, hosting or providing English as a Second Language (ESL) classes so that they can learn how to communicate in English, helping them find employment and learn their new culture and laws, aiding in the process of finding legal assistance,[13] and coming alongside them to assist with the process of becoming a U.S. citizen. Sometimes simply being a friend, like doing things together or grabbing a meal, is enough, especially if they're international college students.[14] With refugees and immigrants particularly, we can implement the two-pronged strategy of compassion tempered with wisdom to welcome, support, invest in, empower, and stand with them, working together with other churches, non-profit agencies, and the government to make it happen.

Pray. Of course, prayer should be part of this whole process from the very beginning. How can we pray as it relates here? Pray for compassion, wisdom, courage, opportunities, and reform; pray for the people, for the ministers and those being ministered to.

Push for Reform. As mentioned, it is my observation that the system is broken as it relates to how we respond to immigration and responding to refugees. As such, reform is desperately needed—reform that is both compassionate and wise. One starting point to consider here is the Evangelical Statement of Principles for Immigration Reform that was crafted in 2012. This is concise document that calls for a bi-partisan solution that respects the God-given dignity of every person, protects the unity of the immediate family, respects the rule of law, guarantees secure national borders, ensures fairness to taxpayers, and establishes a path toward legal status and/or citizenship for those who qualify and who wish to become permanent residents.[15]

In the end, when it comes to serving internationals, rather than being outraged, divisive, ethnocentric, or xenophobic when they come into our communities, we can choose to get right in the middle of things and welcome and love the strangers among us. If we who are God's people are called to love, then we ought to practice love and embrace the opportunity to express the love of God to people, no matter who they are, and reach the nations with the gospel of Jesus Christ for the glory of God in this world and beyond, starting with the people from other nations who now live among us.

Multicultural Churches

The third way we can participate in the mission is to regularly expose ourselves to, and be on mission together with people from, other cultures. A fabulous way of doing this is to be a multicultural church, or at least worship and do ministry with other-culture churches on a regular basis. As a pastor I have always wanted to lead a multicultural church, but so far, I have only been able to plant ideas that will hopefully someday come to be in churches that I have once served. As I write, I am currently not serving as a church pastor but am part of an ethnically diverse congregation not far from my home. My family and I are truly blessed to be part of this community church, and I am now learning firsthand about some dynamics of multicultural church ministry. What I have gleaned over the years about this is briefly summarized below.

First, what do I mean by multicultural church? I appreciate the work done by people like George Yancey and Manuel Ortiz, who have done much to put this into practice for many years. Yancey writes that a multicultural or multiracial church is "a church in which no one racial group makes up more than 80 percent of the attendees of at least one of the major worship services."[16] Ortiz adds that the "goal of the multiethnic church is to urge the body of Christ, in all its diversity, to be Christian, as described in the Bible"[17] and that the "purpose of maintaining the multiethnic church is to establish a church that is committed to seeing Christ reign among his people and to establishing a people of God who are united in their diversity."[18]

Why pursue such a thing? First, the house of God, we're told in the scriptures, is to be a place for all peoples of the earth to gather and pray (see Isaiah 56:6-8, Mark 11:17). This "house of prayer" originally referred to the Temple in Jerusalem, but it is reasonable to extend that identification to the structures we call churches. Our gathering places should therefore be considered as places for all peoples to gather to pray and worship the one true living God. Second, we are consistently encouraged and instructed throughout the scriptures to be the united people of God in this world who testify to the unity of the Trinity and the unity of Christ with

His people in this world (see Psalm 133, John 17:11 & 20-23, Ephesians 4:1-6).

Remember, we are on mission *together* as all of God's people in this world, which is very ethnically and culturally diverse. Third, we know that heaven will include people from all nations and cultures who, among other things, will be worshiping and serving the Lord together for all eternity (see Revelation 7:9-12 & 15:1-4). When we worship with people from other cultures in this life, we are getting a taste of heaven, of God's eternal kingdom—a reality that we regularly pray for in this life, that His kingdom would come on earth as it is in heaven (Matthew 6:10).

Moving forward with this, what are some things to consider? The recipe for success includes the following ingredients. First, *intentional commitment.* If you ask any pastor or church leader, they will tell you how difficult ministry can be. If you ask any pastor or leader of a multicultural church, they will tell you that this type of church ministry is often even more challenging. If this is the direction the Lord is moving you, then a deep level of intentionality and commitment to seeing it happen is needed. Involved with this are such things as establishing a clear, focused, strategic vision that helps to create an environment for it to happen, rather than trying to force or manufacture something for the sake of ego or political correctness. The process will take time, so patience is needed to maintain the right pace. The process will also include learning from one another, addressing cultural barriers, overcoming challenges, and persevering through the many disagreements that will arise, as well as the departure of those who do not agree with being diverse or how the process is going. This is all presuming that there is already a diverse population within the church's community, which we desire to also be seen within the church.

Second, *prayer*. Prayer remains foundational in all that we do, and the pursuit of a multiethnic church is certainly no different as we absolutely need to depend on the guidance of the Holy Spirit to provide us with the unity-in-diversity that we see in the Trinity. Pray for wisdom and guidance every step of the way, asking God to make everything clear, from the time of floating the idea and establishing a vision, to fully implementing the plan to make it happen, to the ongoing expression of unity among God's people who are doing life together.

Third, *warm embrace*. All churches should be safe, hospitable places, whether mono-ethnic or ethnically and culturally diverse. As inclusion is promoted and practiced, and as barriers are deconstructed, we are more able to selflessly love and serve one another as we extend grace and practice forgiveness in the midst of our human condition of brokenness and broken relationships.

Fourth, *relationship*. The key to all of this is found in healthy relationship with God, our selves, and one another. This takes the aspect of warm embrace even further as we seek to be friends who see one another as uniquely created in the image of God. Truly, we are one human race who happens to reflect the incredible creative artistry of the artist who created us. As we think this way and as we practice the type of warm embrace already described, we begin to push through what separates us and move toward acceptance and genuine friendship. We listen to one another, we learn from one another, we resolve our conflicts in healthier ways, and we repent of the wrongs we have done to one other. In a word, we love one another as we should be loved, as family.

Fifth, *inclusive worship and ministry*. Worship gatherings in the multicultural church should, to some degree, manifest the various ethnic and cultural elements that are present in the congregation—in the music that is played, the songs that are sung, and the people who are leading worship. This will likely include a variety of musical styles that will initially stretch the congregation and may involve singing some songs in different languages (it's a good idea to use translators if other language groups are present). This most likely means doing ministry differently and serving the possibly overlooked ethnic groups in the community that may be.

Finally, *diverse leadership*. In a word, pastoral staff and church leadership at all levels in a multiethnic church ought to reflect the different ethnicities and cultural dynamics that are present in the congregation. A multicultural church, in other words, should have multicultural leadership, diverse leaders who are equally empowered to lead as they set the example of what it means to be united in diversity.

Is this kind of pursuit for everybody? The dreamer in me says, "Yes, absolutely!" The realist in me says, "Maybe." It's hard work to make the move to becoming/being a multicultural church, but it is good work that is truly worth it in the end, and it is definitely something that the Lord desires of us. If this does not describe your current church, pray about it and sit down with your pastor and other leaders to see if the Lord may be moving you in this direction. If not, that's okay. This is a good thing to pursue, but it is not mandatory. At least, though, be willing to worship and do ministry with other culture churches on a regular basis. Either way, take these words to heart: "As the church of Jesus Christ resounds with its great symphony of praise on earth as it is in heaven, the world will see and hear a compelling sound of Christian unity. They will read the church as a relevant book of God's love, a unified almanac with one unending story of God's grace and peace."[19]

Be Exposed, Get Experienced

As we desire to get more involved with the work of the mission, we see that there are three strategic ways that we can participate: cross-cultural ministry involvement, serving internationals in the community and region, and being a multicultural church. Much has been written about all these things elsewhere, including many helpful manuals. I strongly suggest that you consult the resources noted at the end of this chapter and this book for more information about how to go further with each of these types of ministry. With much prayer and courage, may we take some steps forward to either begin doing such things or to participate to even greater degrees.

Principle in Practice
Compelled to Love

In Pittsburgh, Pennsylvania, there are many churches that are actively pursuing ministry with refugees and other immigrants throughout the city, and a multidenominational network of churches and organizations working together is growing. One of those churches is a large ethnically diverse congregation on the city's north side known as Allegheny Center Alliance Church (ACAC), a Christian & Missionary Alliance (C&MA) church that has been present in the community for over 100 years. A few years ago, in 2013, the presence of refugees from East Africa and Syria in the community came to the attention of some key missions leaders in the congregation and soon ministry in various ways was underway. The vision for this type of ministry really began to develop further in early 2015 when the church responded to refugee needs by offering ESL classes, which ended up not working too well due to cross-cultural misunderstandings and other related issues.

Soon a couple experienced in cross-cultural ministry overseas that was supported by the church became more actively involved. By the spring of 2016 they were overseeing one of the ministries that was birthed out of ACAC to minister to some of the refugees and they began to meet with leaders of the refugee community to determine what their greatest needs were. As people prayed for this ministry, God answered in some amazing ways. Indeed, as the couple leading this ministry indicate, it was "*God* who orchestrated the timing of things and it was *God* who provided everything that was needed. God's power to meet their needs is what opened the door." Now a couple years later, the ministry known as In the Steps of Boaz continues to rapidly grow as volunteers from nine different churches (including ACAC) build relationships with the refugee community, teach ESL and life skills classes, and conduct various ministry events as opportunities to share the gospel keep presenting themselves, all with the acceptance of the refugees and blessing of their leaders.

While all this was happening, another segment of the refugee population was also being ministered to. Driven particularly by the need to provide counseling and trauma care, Dr. Cathy Sigmund (a C&MA chaplain at ACAC) recruited volunteers to begin doing ministry in a neighborhood not far from the church, all with "the intent to love them," as Dr. Sigmund would say. First contact was made in 2014, and before long, mission posts were established in the community and the growing team of volunteers (from a few different churches) began to teach ESL classes, host community gathering occasions, offer chapel services and other ministry events, provide counseling, and eventually teach naturalization and citizenship classes. Grace Mission, as it's known, is the second ministry to be birthed out of ACAC to help serve refugees and other internationals in their community. This effort has further expanded into other neighborhoods and a network of churches in the region, Embrace Global Care, has begun to collaborate in ministry together to reach the peoples of the world living throughout Western Pennsylvania.

As these two ministries came into being, a third one joined them. The Christian Immigration Advocacy Center (CIAC) was formally established in 2018 after a couple years of prayerful discussion among missions leaders and law professionals at the church about how to help meet the need for immigration legal services. Working together with other organizations in Pittsburgh, CIAC offers limited free legal advice and assistance with such things as non-immigrant visas, green card renewals, naturalization, family reunification, and asylum. Already they are serving over 100 clients in their first year of operation.

Three separate, but related, organizations spawned off and supported by one congregation as a way to serve the internationals in the community. How does this happen? Missions pastor Glenn Hanna suggests that "money is not necessarily needed, just a lot of prayer, wise counsel, planning, and a team of committed volunteers."

Meanwhile, across the city, there is a small church led by Pastor Dan Craner called Zion Christian Church, which is in the middle of another refugee area of Pittsburgh known as "Little Nepal" (because of the heavy presence of Bhutanese and Nepali people). Though they haven't created new organizations to meet refugee and immigrant needs, this small group of people work together with some other area ministries to help meet basic life needs of neighborhood refugees like assist with grocery shopping and acquire furniture, offer ESL and citizenship classes, distribute Bibles and evangelistic material in the relevant language, host Bible studies, and provide opportunities for friendships to develop; Nepali classes are also offered for the English speakers.

The result of this kind of ministry is that Christ is being introduced to the people as trust is established and love is exhibited. This is seen especially with the children who have started coming to Sunday school and other church activities. They are the most responsive and receptive and are the most common focus in ministry. While not everyone in the church has caught the vision for such ministry, there is a growing group of core people that has. Some of them have even traveled to Nepal to minister to Bhutanese refugees there, which only furthers the relationships here. It is a vision and a ministry that Pastor Craner is absolutely set to keep before the people. In his words, "The refugees are a huge part of my life and the life of the church."

Two churches, one city, different neighborhoods—both reaching internationals in their community. Large or small, all those involved would say that all it takes is a lot of prayer, a love devoted to caring for and befriending people, a vision for the gospel reaching all peoples, and a team of committed volunteers to help make it happen. "The need is there," Pastor Craner says. "Other groups are coming to the United States and the landscape is changing. This is a huge mission field."

Pray, Love, Serve

Cornerstone Christian Fellowship is a small Christian & Missionary Alliance church in the Columbus suburb of Hilliard, Ohio, that is fast becoming more and more multicultural as the community in which it ministers becomes more and more ethnically diverse. Led by pastors Jonathan and Irma Chon, Cornerstone has a vision that was born out of prayer to reach the nations that have come to Hilliard, especially those who are Muslims. How are they doing this? Through missional living, establishing relationships, and cultivating friendships with the people with whom they come in contact. What started as the church simply having a presence at the local farmer's market by way of selling baked goods has become a growing ministry with many chances to serve.

Each week, for example, there are meetings at the church where people gather to just practice conversations in English. And there's the first Friday of each month when the ladies get together to eat, practice English, and even teach one another different cultural things. The men have their time, too, when they get together as fathers and sons to play soccer in a soccer league. All of this, along with occasional special outreaches, are serving as opportunities for people to be loved, relationships to be built, and the gospel to be presented. Serving Hilliard's international population in this way, Pastor Irma says, "opens doors to share Christ and provides opportunities to pray." And this has not gone unnoticed by the people that Cornerstone is serving, as the women especially are seeing answers to the prayers of God's people. To be clear, this is not the pet project of the pastors of Cornerstone, not is it the ministry of just a few. This is "a vision and ministry that," according to Pastor Irma, "the whole church has caught and put into practice."

Unplanned Multicultural Blessing

When Covenant Community Church, a smaller Presbyterian (PCA) church in the Pittsburgh suburb of Wexford, Pennsylvania, started becoming more multicultural, it was not by design; rather, it was what Pastors Jon Price and Alex Martinez call a "God-ordained thing done in response to a need that was discovered in the community." At one time, Covenant Community Church was your typical monocultural American church that was supportive of missions, and they were content with that. All that changed in 2012, when Jon noticed that there was a growing Hispanic population in his community and he invited his Mexican brother-in-law, Alex, to join the staff as Assistant Pastor of Worship and Multicultural Ministries.

Soon after Alex joined the staff, he and his family were eating at a local Chinese restaurant when they met a group of Guatemalan people who approached him and asked if he would lead a Bible study for them. Needless to say, they began meeting regularly in 2013 and some began to attend the church. Soon the pastors and elders were asked about the possibility of creating a Spanish-speaking service, or at least including Spanish in the worship services. In early 2014 this became a reality, first as an occasional Spanish-speaking service but eventually as a regular bi-lingual worship experience that incorporated singing in both English and Spanish and involving real-time translators. Soon the greater Hispanic community, consisting of Guatemalans, Cubans, Mexicans, El Salvadorans, Peruvians, and Hondurans, were invited to participate and the congregation began to see what else could be done as they started taking steps to becoming more intentionally multicultural. "This process did not happen quickly or without difficulty," Pastor Price is quick to say, "we did what we could do until we could more fully minister to these people, and we are still in transition." Truly, they have followed the Lord's lead to more fully serve their diverse community and by the fall of 2016 they expanded beyond Spanish and bi-lingual worship and started offering ESL classes for those who need to learn English and Spanish classes for those who need to learn Spanish. "Overall," Pastors Price and Martinez submit, "this change has been positive and well-received by our people, who see this as a way to bless the nations as we continue to discover what it means to practice biblical hospitality."

Suggested Resources

Steve Corbett and Brian Fikkert. *Helping Without Hurting in Short-Term Missions*. Chicago: Moody Press, 2014.

David A. Livermore. *Serving with Eyes Wide Open: Doing Short-Term Missions with Cultural Intelligence*. Updated ed. Grand Rapids: Baker Books, 2013.

Roger Peterson et al. *Maximum Impact Short-Term Mission*. Minneapolis: STEM Press, 2003.

Ellen Livingood. *Your Focus on the World: A Step-by-Step Guide to Leading Your Whole Church into Maximum Global Impact*. Newtown: Catalyst Services, (available at www.catalystservices.org)

David Wesley. *A Common Mission: Healthy Patterns in Congregational Mission Partnerships*. Eugene: Resource Publications, 2014.

Rajendra K. Pillai. *Reaching the World in Our Own Backyard*. Colorado Springs: Waterbrook Press, 2003.

Kathleen Leslie et al. *Church Leader's Guide to Immigration*. Baltimore: World Relief, 2014.

Matthew Soerens and Jenny Yang. *Welcoming the Stranger: Justice, Compassion & Truth in the Immigration Debate*. Revised and expanded. Downers Grove: IVP Books, 2018.

Tom Phillips et al. *The World at Your Door: Reaching International Students in Your Home, Church, and School*. Minneapolis: Bethany House Publishers, 1997.

David A. Anderson. *Multicultural Ministry: Finding Your Church's Unique Rhythm*. Grand Rapids: Zondervan, 2004.

George Yancey. *One Body One Spirit: Principles of Successful Multiracial Churches*. Downers Grove: InterVarsity Press, 2003.

Notes

[1] David Platt, *Radical: Taking Back Your Faith from the American Dream* (Colorado Springs: Multnomah Books, 2010), 198.

[2] Enoch Wan, "The Phenomenon of Diaspora: Missiological Implications for Christian Missions," in *Asian American Christianity: A Reader*, ed. Viji Nakka-Cammauf and Timothy Tseng (Castro Valley: The Institute for the Study of Asian American Christianity, 2009), 157.

[3] Though short-term missions experiences are not the main focus of this book, some important issues concerning these experiences (i.e., the tension of process vs. project, the benefits and drawbacks of short-term missions experiences, and the impact of short-term missions on long-term missions involvement) merit some discussion, which are taken up in Appendix D.

[4] Paul Borthwick, *Youth and Missions: Expanding Your Students' Worldview*, 2nd ed.

(Waynesboro, GA: OM Literature, 1998), 139. It should be noted here that many members of the younger generations (Millennials and Generation Z) are already poised for such experiences because of their ethnic diversity and because they tend to be globally-minded, experience-oriented risk takers who already have friends all over the world (thanks to social media) and who enjoy operating in extreme situations. Furthermore, they also tend to shy away from anything long-term, wanting first to sample and explore something before making any kind of commitment to it.

[5] Another type of experience would simply be a cross-cultural learning experience that is used primarily to either educate students or to develop a deeper level of commitment or discipleship in trip participants. This would result in some exposure to missions and may involve some ministry but would not be considered a ministry-driven opportunity or even a missions trip (since it benefits the participant more than the nationals). It should be noted here that challenging people to live the Christ life does not necessarily require participation in short-term missions experiences in order

for spiritual growth to occur. Though involvement in ministry is part of this process for all Christians, doing it cross-culturally is not mandatory.

[6] In my opinion, a goal each church (or collection of churches) should have is to enter into at least one ministry partnership in every continent or region of the world, ideally with people they are already in relationship with when possible.

[7] For clarity's sake, some definitions will be helpful here. Immigrants/ Migrants "choose to move not because of a direct threat of persecution or death, but mainly to improve their lives by finding work, or in some cases for education, family reunion, or other reasons…If they choose to return home, they will continue to receive the protection of their government." (United Nations. "UNHCR Viewpoint: 'Refugee' or 'migrant'—Which Is Right?" UNHCR. July 11, 2016. Accessed November 23, 2018.https://www.unhcr.org/ news/latest/2016/7/55d-f0e556/unhcr-viewpoint-refugee-migrant-right.html); migrants tend to be temporary or seasonal, immigrants typically plan to stay long-term or permanently. A refugee, on the other hand, "is a person who is outside his or her country of nationality or last habitual residence and is unable or unwilling to return to that country because of persecution or a well-founded fear of persecution on account of race, religion, nationality, membership in a particular social group, or political opinion." (U.S. Departments of State, Homeland Security, and Health and Human Services, "Proposed Refugee Admissions for Fiscal Year 2012 Report to the Congress," October 20, 2011, 14)

[8] In my travels to various places in the world, this is certainly not a problem unique to the U.S.—many countries are encountering the same situations and engaging in the same discussions.

[9] See Genesis 45:4-8, Deuteronomy 32:8, and Acts 17:26-28.

[10] See Leviticus 19:9-18 & 33-34, Deuteronomy 10:17-19, Micah 6:8, Zechariah 7:8-10, Matthew 5:43-48 & 22:34-40, Mark 12:28-34, Luke 10:25-37, Romans 12:9-13 & 13:8-10, Galatians 5:14, Hebrews 13:1-2, and James 2:1-13.

[11] See Acts 5:27-29, Romans 13:1-7, 1 Peter 2:13-17

[12]Imagine the global impact of the gospel when international students (as well as business people and migrant workers who are in our community for a short time) become followers of Jesus who return to their homeland as evangelists and disciple makers for God's kingdom! Many times, when we invest in them here, they return home bringing the gospel with them to places where we ourselves may not be welcome—another way for the mission to be accomplished around the world.

[13]Consider becoming an immigration legal site via the U.S. Department of Justice's Recognition & Accreditation Program—go to www. justice.gov/eoir/recognition-and-accreditation-program; also reach out to The Immigration Alliance (www.theimmigrationalliance.org) for further assistance.

[14]Full disclosure: ministry with immigrants and refugees, especially Muslims and undocumented people, will not likely be popular, at least not at first (and at least in the Western world); in fact, there may be a significant price to pay. For such ministry to happen, it will take love, humility, patience, a lot of time, a commitment to learn, and quite possibly repenting of idols that we may have that relate to nationalism, tribalism, and racial bias. (Thanks to scholar Matthew Kaemingk who gently nudged me to remember this when I attended a workshop of his at the Acton University conference in 2018; I highly recommend his book that addresses this quite well—*Christian Hospitality and Muslim Immigration in an Age of Fear* (Grand Rapids: Eerdmans Publishing Co., 2018))

[15]The statement may be found at http://evangelicalimmigrationtable. com/.

[16]George Yancey, *One Body One Spirit* (Downers Grove: InterVarsity Press, 2003), 15.

[17]Manuel Ortiz, *One New People* (Downers Grove: InterVarsity Press, 1996), 25.

[18]Ibid., 130.

[19]David A. Anderson, *Multicultural Ministry* (Grand Rapids: Zondervan, 2004), 24-25.

CHAPTER 8

CHURCH LEADERSHIP
AND MISSION

"The secret of enabling the home Church to press her ad-
vantage in the non-Christian world is one of leadership.
The people do not go beyond their leaders in knowledge
and zeal, nor surpass them in consecration and sacri-
fice. The Christian pastor, minister, rector...holds the
divinely appointed office for inspiring and guiding the
thought and activities of the Church... Wherever you
find a pastor with overflowing missionary zeal and
knowledge, you will find an earnest missionary church."[1]

- John R. Mott -

"[Pastoral] missions involvement makes for a stronger local
assembly."[2]

- Vaughn J. Walston -

It cannot be overstated that each local church should encourage a year-round missions climate where missions is integrated into everyone's way of life. As someone who has served in some kind of pastoral ministry role for nearly twenty-five years, I know the importance of this, and many of my pastor colleagues do, too. What troubles me is knowing that there are many more pastors and local churches across the country that seem to be minimally interested in missions, if they're interested at all.

As a missions mobilizer, I have made it a goal of mine to fix this, because pastors and other church leaders are in incredible positions of influence in the lives of people. As such, the process of encouraging people in our churches to understand and embrace the task set before us by Jesus to evangelize and make disciples around the world (beginning in one's own community) begins with church leadership, especially the pastor.

Consider the words of Rev. Dr. George Pentecost at the Ecumenical Missionary Conference of 1900 in New York City,

> To the pastor belongs the privilege and the responsibility of solving the missionary problem. Until the pastors of our churches wake to the truth of this proposition, and the foreign work of the Church becomes a passion in their hearts and consciences...the chariot wheels of foreign missions will drive heavily... If there are churches that give not and pray not for foreign missions, it is because they have pastors who are false and [unfaithful] to the command of Christ.[3]

Consider also the words of S. Earl Taylor, who in 1900 was the Organizer of Campaign Work among Young People in the USA, who shared this sentiment at the same missionary conference, "Until our pastors are ready to back this enterprise, there will never be a missionary spirit adequate to the needs of this generation."[4] Also at this missionary conference, Yale Band's D. Brewer Eddy, while speaking about giving money to the work of missions, further added that the "importance of leadership must be emphasized...You are the leader[s]. We...young people...are willing to follow you, if you will guide us."[5]

So, a major key to developing and maintaining a year-round missions climate is the pastor and other leaders of the church, who together create a vision for the worldwide work of Christ. When the pastor and church leadership are committed to and enthusiastic about missions, the people of the congregation are more likely to increase their involvement and commitment level; if such leadership is not provided, the church will lack the direction that is needed.

Leading the Way

While the key person of influence is the senior pastor, he does not stand alone. The responsibility lies with all of the church's leadership. The global vision of the pastor should bleed over to other church staff pastors and members, church elders, and various ministry leaders. They then help the pastor lead the way for the congregation to live *on mission* together. The suggestions that follow, therefore, apply to the senior pastor as well as other church leader. How, then, can pastors and church leaders lead the way?

First, they should read and study the Bible to know what the *whole* Bible says about God's global heart and how He has acted throughout history around the world, from creation to the restoration that is yet to come. The Bible should also be carefully and prayerfully studied to more fully understand what our work of worldwide evangelism and disciplemaking is all about. It's not enough to know just the "Great Commission" or to choose one or two favorite verses or passages of scripture; pastors and church leaders especially should be familiar with the full teaching of scripture here.

It would be good for pastors and church leaders to also read missions-related material, so that they become more familiar with the history of missions since the New Testament era. This includes reading biographies of missionaries, missions theology resources, and even overviews of missions strategy and practice.

As insight into missions is gleaned from the Bible, theology, and history, it is important to pass on this knowledge to others so that they, too, are educated about missions. Pastor John Piper explained it well,

> From time to time in the life of the church, it becomes crucial that pastors rehearse the essential truths about missions that feed a passion for God's supremacy among the nations. Why do we care so much about missions? The people need to hear this. And what is it anyway? Many Christians are oblivious of the most glorious story in world history, the spread of Christianity through the blood and tears and joy of world missions.[6]

Educating people about missions, though, is not enough. Pastors and church leaders can also dedicate themselves to motivating people toward missions as they invest in them and help them grow as disciples. In fact, pastors and church leaders are even more important than missionaries in this respect. Most, if not all, missionaries would likely agree. One of my missionary friends, who shall remain anonymous due to the nature of his ministry, has publicly said it this way: "We need pastors who will mobilize people and raise up disciples and people who will be missionaries."

There are several ways to do this. One way is to be intentional about integrating missions into *all* areas of ministry programming in the church, always casting the vision for people to be outward-focused and missional with their lives while training and equipping them to do so locally, regionally, and globally. Other ways include publicly praying for missions in corporate worship gatherings, preaching and teaching about missions, publicly promoting missions activities and involvement while showing personal investment, persuading people in the congregation to pray for and to give to the work of missions, urging people to be active in sending new missionaries, and exhorting people to consider becoming vocational missionaries themselves.

Another priority for church leadership in relation to missions is to invest in the next generation. It should be noted here that Millennials and younger generations are more racially and ethnically diverse, with many who are willing to emigrate and work internationally or cross-culturally. They are already attuned to an international mindset and would fit well in a non-Western Church setting. Pastors, especially, should confront them with their responsibility to evangelize this generation of people currently alive around the world; younger generations need to be challenged to see where they fit in to God's global plan. As this happens, it is important to realize that such investment in young people should begin when they are children, not when they become teenagers. It would even benefit to have young people directly involved with leading church missions programming and ministries.

Finally, pastors and church leaders ought to lead by example, modeling excitement about missions and missional living while praying for missions, giving to missions, and personally participating in missions. It is critical for church leadership to set the right tone for living on mission together. John R. Mott, founder and key leader of the Student Volunteer Movement of the early 20th century, conveyed this sentiment well in his book, *The Pastor and Modern Missions*,

> The pastor is the director general of the Christian forces. He should regard his church not alone as a field to be cultivated, but also and more especially as a force to be wielded on behalf of the evangelization of the world...What is an army without a leader? But the leader must himself know the way, must keep ahead, and must get others to follow as a result of his own courageous spirit and contagious earnestness...The pastor is not only a leader of his members at home, but an advocate for the people abroad. If he does not plead their cause, who will? The multitude of the distant nations cannot come to seek for themselves, even were they conscious of their need. Nor can the missionary do so. The missionary visitor may arouse temporary interest. But it is the missionary pastor who make a church a missionary power the year through.[7]

Pastoral Involvement

As the pastor, along with other church leaders, leads the way toward missional living, it is important that he be directly involved with the work of cross-cultural ministry, not just local church ministry. On the surface, this may seem like such involvement does not have any relevance to the local church or the pastorate, especially in a small church. However, with easier, less time-consuming travel in our society, is there any reason for the pastor not to be involved?

Perhaps you're asking yourself, "Why should my pastor be doing ministry with people on the other side of the world when he has enough ministry to do here at my church and in our community?" That's a fair question. But consider something very important here: The pastor sets the tone for and models ministry in the church, including engagement in missions. It is the pastor who sets the prime example and he should therefore lead by example. When pastors lead the way for missions, their own heart is ignited with a passion for God's global work, and they are better grounded in reaching a lost world for Christ. This fire then spreads throughout the congregation.

A pastor's involvement with cross-cultural ministry also allows him to help members of the congregation find their role in missions, too, especially if short-term missions is part of the church's overall strategy for missions mobilization. Plus, the connections with international workers and national churches are strengthened because of the pastor's direct involvement, which is especially important for churches involved with a cross-cultural ministry partnership.

The church also benefits greatly here. As the congregation's view of the world and the need for Christ around the world is further enhanced, and as more personal connections are made with missionaries and people from other cultures, the people become more personally connected to the *missio Dei*. As a result, prayer for missions expands, giving to missions increases, and missional engagement becomes a credible and practical reality. As the church becomes more outward-focused in this way, global outreach ministry actually fuels local and regional outreach ministry. The people get more excited not just about global missions, but also local evangelism.

It's important to reinforce here, the need for help in this area. While the pastor may be the primary leader, he cannot do it alone. Not only does he need other church staff and ministry leaders, but he also needs a good Missions Mobilization

Team because strong, committed, passionate leadership is part of the key to seeing the church's global vision come to be. Again, every local church should have such a team in place to help provide leadership in the area of generating missions awareness throughout the year in all of the church's ministry programs. The pastor should *not* be doing this alone. He needs help to intentionally design a strategic process for making disciples of all people everywhere, not just in the church's community but also throughout the world. At the same time, the pastor should not relegate this leadership to the Missions Mobilization Team or other church staff alone. He needs to remain actively involved in the process in some way. For further insight into leading with a team, please reread this section of Chapter 3.

Invitation to Lead

If we want our people to become more globally aware and become involved with missions, then it must begin first with those of us who are the leaders within the church, especially the pastor. When we set the tone and become involved ourselves, the people will follow. The opportunities and resources, both human and financial, are available like never before in history. Now is the time to really lead the people forward in mission, loving God and loving others in every sense of the word. May we who are leaders, lead.

Principle in Practice

One Pastor's Influence

"I have always been a missions enthusiast," Ted Martin says, and every church where he has served as pastor has taken note of that. In 2007 he became the pastor of Hampton Presbyterian Church in Gibsonia, Pennsylvania, a large mainline

Presbyterian congregation that, despite a legacy of missions support, only financially supported missions in the years prior to Pastor Martin's arrival with money left over at the end of the year. Although the youth would go on an annual summer missions trip, the adults were removed from hands-on missions engagement themselves. In fact, Ted would tell you, "missions was on the back burner in terms of being considered a priority, financially or otherwise." Soon after he began serving there, he began working with the church's missions committee to change that—to make God's mission a priority in their community, throughout their region, and to the ends of the earth.

Before long, the church was giving 10% of their budget (as "first fruits") four times each year to twelve international and twelve domestic missionaries with whom the church has a relationship and whose work is in alignment with Hampton Presbyterian's values and ministry desires. The committee also began to host an annual missions focus Sunday that features the traditional missions décor and displays while allowing each of their supported domestic missionaries to speak briefly about their work and what God is doing through their ministry; international workers are given opportunities to speak any time they happen to be in the area.

What makes this story especially noteworthy is that Pastor Martin has, in recent years, used part of his sabbatical grant to allow a pastor (and family) from a partner church in Malawi to enjoy a sabbatical retreat, and he regularly uses his study leave and allowance each year to go visit with the church's supported workers around the world to personally provide support, encouragement, and pastoral care for them. He has also led 14 different short-term ministry trips for adults from the church and he indicates that he is "trying to figure out a way to get people's employers to free them to do these kinds of trips without penalty of any kind (like using vacation time, [or] docking pay)."

The youth of the congregation have continued to be involved with short-term ministry opportunities as well, so much so that the senior high group has an intentional three-year cycle of experiences that include one year of equipping for ministry, one domestic trip, and one experience overseas. As a result of this pastor's influence, this congregation no longer sees missions as something to occasionally talk about. This group of inspired people has instead been stirred to more fully engage in the mission that God has set before them.

Pastor as Mobilizer

First Reformed Presbyterian (RPCNA) Church in Beaver Falls, Pennsylvania is a small congregation made up of all generations, all types of professions, and some college students. It is also a church with a long history of missions involvement and being directly connected with missionaries in various places in the world, people that they support both financially and with consistent prayer. They currently have a family that they have personally sent serving in South Sudan as missionaries. This group of around 100 people do not see their small size as being an obstacle at all as it relates to missions.

This begins to make sense when one realizes the pastoral influence that has existed here. One former pastor, for example, had himself been a missionary and taught missions at the Reformed Presbyterian Theological Seminary in nearby Pittsburgh. It's fair to say that part of the fruit of his ministry was the groundwork that he was unknowingly laying for such strong commitment to missions to happen.

The church's current pastor, Lucas Hanna, was himself a missionary briefly in South Sudan before returning to the United States to do ministry here as a pastor and a missions mobilizer who does what he can to remain involved overseas. For two months each year, he returns to South Sudan as a worker funded by the RP Global (the missionary arm of the Reformed Presbyterian Church of North America) to teach two different intensive courses to train national workers and provide pastoral care for the church's missionary family in a direct and personal way.

Pastor Hanna is quick to tell you that he is "very intentional about caring for the people in his congregation, even if they are on the other side of the world." The church is equally intentional about supporting his ministry, so much so that they brought Pastor Hanna and his family to the church with the clear understanding that would fully support his ministry as their pastor and his ongoing work in South Sudan and beyond; their only concern is for his family when he is away, an aspect that is always being re-examined out of genuine love and concern for the whole family.

This church has an associate pastor as well, Matt Filbert, who regularly communicates the vision and work of missions and the church's involvement with it. Matt also serves as the Director of RP Missions, the short-term missions arm of the denomination, which often translates into short-term missions ministry teams being sent from the church. Together these pastors and other church leaders work hard to lead and inspire the people while modeling an involvement with missions which then directly impacts the whole congregation, fully engaging them in the ministry of missions around the world, beginning in their own community and region. According to Pastor Filbert, this kind of participation "moves missions from the hypothetical to the practical in our church. It makes missions real." Both pastors would wholeheartedly agree that such leadership is needed in every local church.

Suggested Resources

Richard R. Deridder & Roger S. Greenway. *Let the Whole World Know: Resources for Preaching on Missions*. Grand Rapids: Baker Publishing Group, 1988.

David Horner. *When Missions Shape the Mission: You and Your Church Can Reach the World*. Nashville: B&H Publishing Group, 2011.

John R. Mott. *The Pastor and Modern Missions: A Plea for Leadership in World Evangelization*. New York: Student Volunteer Movement for Foreign Missions, 1904.

John Piper. *Brothers, We Are Not Professionals: A Plea to Pastors for Radical Ministry*, updated and expanded ed. Nashville: Broadman & Holman Publishers, 2015.

(Chapter 31)

Ralph D. Winter and Steven C. Hawthorne, eds. *Perspectives on the World Christian Movement: A Reader*. 4th ed. Pasadena: William Carey Library, 2009.

Notes

[1] John R. Mott, *The Pastor and Modern Missions: A Plea for Leadership in World Evangelization* (New York: Student Volunteer Movement for Foreign Missions, 1904), vii and 51.

[2] Vaughn Walston, "Mobilizing the African-American Church for Global Evangelization," in *African-American Experience in World Mission: A Call Beyond Community*, 2nd ed., ed. Vaughn J. Walston and Robert J. Stevens (Pasadena: William Carey Library, 2009), 189.

[3] Quoted in Bliss et al., *Ecumenical Missionary Conference, New York, 1900: Report of the Ecumenical Conference on Foreign Missions* (New York: American Tract Society, 1900), 125-126, 130.

[4] Ibid., 141.

[5] Ibid., 181-182.

[6] John Piper, *Brothers, We Are Not Professionals* (Nashville: Broadman & Holman Publishers, 2002), 188-89.

[7] Mott, 52-53.

CHAPTER 9

FUTURE MISSIONARIES

"The harvest is great, but the workers are few. So, pray to the Lord who is in charge of the harvest; ask him to send more workers into his fields."[1]

- Jesus Christ -

"Each of us has a key role to play supporting and serving an emerging generation of world-changing followers of Jesus. To be able to achieve their full potential, they need us to stand with them, cheering them on, providing affirmation and solidarity. Christians of all ages need to pray for them, mentor them, encourage them, equip them, protect them, and allow them to lead."[2]

- David Wraight -

I am in the business of developing people. As a pastor, an educator, and a missions mobilizer, I am motivated to teach and influence those entrusted to my care. In the end, anyone who is a leader is to some degree in the same kind of relational investment and influence. If we are leading and influencing the people in our churches to be engaged in missions, doing everything we can to make them aware of the work of God around the world while encouraging them to pray, give, and get personally involved, then we surely will be focused not just on sending out workers and caring for them but also on how we can identify and raise up the next generation or two of vocational missionaries who will serve the Lord in various places around the world.

In our time, at least in the West, the younger generations naturally seem more attuned to the possibilities of this kind of service. They are ethnically diverse and globally-minded, making it more feasible to fit well within a non-Western context and ministry setting. This means tapping into this global interest and working hard to develop a missions climate within every local church, beginning in our children's ministry programs and continuing throughout our years of ministering to teenagers, college students, and young adults.

Early on, during the formative years, it is imperative that our children and teenagers be exposed to God's mission and our partnership with it as they are encouraged, even urged, to evangelize the people within their community and around the world. Indeed, it would be good practice for us to challenge them to see where they fit in to God's global plan as their vocational path intersects with the invitation to join God's people in being on mission together. How do we do this? What are some things that we can do to help foster such a mindset? What do we do when people start responding to the "missionary call"?

Understanding Calling

A good place to start is to understand what "calling" means, especially in this era of people getting hung up with, and even paralyzed by, trying to figure out what to do with their lives. So, let's back up and get some insight into what this means, which will then help us help others. Knowing why we're here begins with first knowing what our identity is.

Simply put, each of us is created uniquely in the image of God, and those who follow Jesus are further being re-created in the image of Christ. Our identity as God's people is found not in what we do, but rather in who we are and Who we belong to. Knowing this, and being comfortable with that, frees us to know how to then live and behave, and it brings us such things as confidence, sharper thinking skills, stability in life, faith, courage, and friendliness toward others as we seek to live in a way that pleases God. With this in mind, we can better explore what it is that God calls each of us to be and to do.

A journey through the scriptures reveals many things about our sense of calling in life. We can condense it all to two things that the Lord calls us to. We are called first to salvation, holiness, and submitting to the lordship of Jesus Christ.[3] We are called second to serve people, wherever it is that God has us and leads us at any given time and place.[4] More simply, each of us is called to love God entirely (heart, soul, mind, strength) and to love people in practical ways.[5]

The late John Stott said it well, noting that calling involves maintaining "Christ's standards of justice, righteousness, honesty, human dignity and compassion in a society which no longer accepts them."[6] Theologian Os Guinness adds further that calling is "the truth that God calls us to himself so decisively that everything we are, everything we do, and everything we have is invested with a special devotion and dynamism lived out as a response to his summons and ser-vice."[7] This is what each of us are called to do as we follow Jesus in this life. It is the calling that all of us have in com-mon, no matter who we are, where we're from, what our back-ground is, how much money we have, how much education we have received, or what our job happens to be.

But what about specific calls for individuals? How does one know what God's preferred desires are for life in terms of how and where to serve? First, let's note that every job and occupation is a holy calling—ministry is for everybody, not just the so-called professionals.[8] Second, let's also realize that some are specially called to what we consider to be vocational ministry, usually as pastors and missionaries. As noted pre-viously, this is our prayer, that the Lord of the Harvest would raise up such people. So, how then do we know for ourselves? And how do we help others recognize such a specific call in their lives (in this case as a sent one rather than a sender)?

Discerning the specifics may be determined within three key relationships: God, one's self, and one's church family. Of utmost importance is to *know God* and be in relationship with Him, learning to know the voice of Jesus the Shepherd while letting the Holy Spirit take the lead. Developing and pursuing this relationship through prayer, worship, and time spent in God's Word will result in His passions and desires becoming our passions and desires. We also need to *know ourselves* and how God has created us in terms of personality, passions, preferences, skills and abilities, talents, preferences, and spiritual gifts. Knowing ourselves includes also paying attention to circumstances and experiences in our lives, as well as seeking advice and insight from those closest to us. This leads to *knowing our church family* and allowing them to know us as the community of faith often helps us discern the call and activity of the Holy Spirit.

As we help people with this kind of discernment, and as God answers our prayers for more workers, we can't just leave them alone to figure out next steps themselves. They need our help, especially if they realize such a calling when they are young.

Mentoring the Called

Coming alongside those called to living on mission cross-culturally involves a process of investment which is relational at its core. Those who express a desire for greater missions involvement and who sense that they may be called to become a missionary should be personally followed-up with and connected with mentors, or at least coaches, who will come alongside them to build an intentional relationship with them and help them be who God created them to be, in this case missionaries. It is imperative that such a process takes place so that future missionaries are sent in a healthy way.[9]

Just as Jesus and Paul did in the first century, these mentors will affirm and inspire them, provide instruction and guidance for them, stimulate and encourage their ambitions, listen to their problems, give them advice and constructive criticism, provide accountability, stretch them and push them to the next level, pray for them and with them, model a Christlike, moral, and family-focused life, show them how to do ministry and help them develop and hone ministry skills, process "on-the-job-training" experiences with them, and send them to serve in ministry on their own.[10]

Along the way, as the relationship develops, mutual personal and spiritual growth occurs as the following areas are impacted and refined: calling and vocation, the heart and one's character, the soul and spiritual formation, the mind and understanding worldview and what one believes, and basics of leadership and ministry practice.

A mentor does not have to be a pastor or ministry leader. A mentor needs only to be a flexible, patient, and caring Christ-follower who is willing to commit to this kind of relationship and offer what has been learned from his or her own experience to a moldable person who desires to serve the Lord. For children, teens, and young adults, these mentors should be adults (pastors, youth pastors and leaders, and missionaries) who will invest in the next generations in this capacity.

Connecting the Called

Aside from mentor-protégé relationships, there are other ways that we can further have an impact on those called, both within these relationships and generally as congregations, ministry leaders, and family members. Here are five areas where we can better connect people with their calling to vocational missions.

Resources. One way to help called ones is to set them up with various missions-related resources like missions books, biographies and autobiographies of missionaries, and websites that are devoted to God's work of mission around the world. Encouraging them to attend missions conferences like the tri-annual Urbana Student Missions Conference and other relevant events are also helpful. Remember, as important as such events are, such things really should serve only to enhance and expand what is already happening within such relationships.

We can also make use of and leverage technology in a way that is relevant, especially for Millennials and Generation Z, by making use of movies, short videos, and social media outlets.

Ministry Opportunities. Any time we can get people involved with local, regional, and global ministry efforts, especially when they're peer-to-peer, the better it will be in their growth, formation, and preparation process for later vocational ministry. For more insight into this, revisit Chapter 7. As mentioned there, this will help them become more outward-focused and not so self-centered while they are challenged to love God and love others while living in obedience to the Great Commission.

Peers. Another helpful thing is to help foster connections between those called with like-minded peers who have also been called to vocational missions or who want to be more involved with missions. One way to see this happen is to have them participate in relevant conferences to facilitate such connections, but also to host or encourage regional and local one-day events that help serve the same purpose by addressing things such as calling, understanding missions, and what is involved in the process of becoming a missionary. Another way to help develop relationships with peers is to gather them together with smaller groups of others who are the same age on a regular basis to encourage and support one another, be accountable to one another, study scripture together, read and discuss missions-related books together, pray for one another and for missions, meet with missionaries and pastors, and just have fun with one another. This could happen with a group from your church or with other future missionaries in your region and should be driven by the needs of the group. This could also be another way to do some group mentoring in addition to what happens one-on-one. This kind of small group peer connection is especially effective with those who are in upper elementary school, middle school, high school, and college.

Missionaries. Remembering the importance of relationships, another great connection for those called to minister cross-culturally is with active or retired missionaries. Those who have served in this capacity already have much that they can pass on to those who are yet to be formally sent. They have already walked the road and can speak from experience about both the blessings and the challenges that come with such ministry. Veteran missionaries are great sounding boards and often make great mentors. Consider also the idea of future missionaries being apprenticed to current missionaries to assist in their journey to the nations. In situations where we can help make that happen, we should do what we can to make it so.

Sending Agencies. One final connection that we can help with at the church end of things is to expose those called to vocational missions to missionary sending agencies, whether that is your denomination or one of countless parachurch agencies. That may mean doing some homework on our part to know what's out there and to be able to recommend agencies that we know and trust. That also means at least sending candidates their way or serving as the bridge to connect the parties involved. When an agency is decided upon, we can also then help people pursue service with said agency, building it into the process of coming alongside them in their journey.

Two Things to Consider

There are two other things that are worth having potential future missionaries consider as they pursue their call to vocational ministry: the idea of not getting married and the idea of working bi-vocationally as a "tentmaker" missionary. Using Jesus and Paul as our guides, let's look briefly at each in turn.

Staying Single. Looking at the scriptures, we see that in all four Gospels Jesus was not married, while 1 Corinthians 7:7-8 reveals that Paul also was not married. While neither of them demanded that Christians should remain single, both taught that marriage was given by God as something good that should be honored and pursued by people. They both nevertheless showed with their lives the principle of remaining unmarried for the sake of ministry. Jesus indicated in Matthew 19:10-12 that remaining single allows a person to live solely for ministering in God's kingdom. Paul taught the same concept in 1 Corinthians 7:25-26 and 32-35, suggesting that being unmarried gives freedom to serve the Lord without the cares and commitments of other relationships being in the way.

Considering this as an option is challenging to say the least, but it is an option that is based on principle, not mandate. Again, neither Jesus nor Paul commanded that all Christians should remain single for the sake of ministry, which would be a spiritual gift; they merely suggested an idea that is worth some consideration by those who sense they are called to vocational ministry. Could it be that some of our children and youth are not meant to be married so that they can pour themselves into ministry in a way that allows them to worry less about time and commitment for family for the sake of the cause? If so, our prayerful guidance will be needed by them.

Working Bi-Vocationally. Another insight to be gained here is the idea of bi-vocational ministry. The most notable example of this is found in Acts 18:1-5, where we read that the apostle Paul needed to generate some income and ministry support by employing himself as a tentmaker, or artisan. In 2 Thessalonians 3:8 he makes his reason for doing this very clear, saying that he and his companions worked hard night and day so as not to be a burden to those whom they were ministering to. As with remaining unmarried in order to serve the Lord, Paul does not command Christians (or missionaries) to be bi-vocational. Rather, he provides an option to be considered and an example that can be followed.

In today's world, this is strategic for two reasons. First, in places where a church has not yet been established and a paid position as a pastor or church planter is less likely or even existent, being bi-vocational provides a legitimate reason and platform for ministering to people in non-threatening ways that also contributes to the common good of the community where the Lord has placed workers. A second reason is the reality that it is dangerous to openly live as a Christ-follower and to publicly do the work of ministry and serving bi-vocationally or in a way where someone is engaged primarily in education or the marketplace is a necessary means of serving in such places. This is usually referred to as "tentmaking" ministry (see Paul's example) or "business as mission," which I am using synonymously here for simplicity's sake. Patrick Lai describes it this way:

> Tentmaking is about a way of revealing God's glory to the ends of the earth...The objective of tentmaking is to put Jesus in front of those who have never had an opportunity to hear the truth about Him, or who have turned their backs on Him because of an encounter with some form of "Christian religion."... Tentmaking is using daily-life strategies to tell people about Jesus. The models and methods vary, but the goal is to glorify Jesus among the unreached.
>
> Tentmakers are determined to build roads through or around the walls which have blocked the spread of cross-cultural discipleship and church planting in the least-reached corners of the world. If the church is to see new churches planted in hostile environments, it must break new ground and build new foundations...Tentmaking is *ministry* outside the box AND *business* outside the box.[11]

Factoring all this in, and remembering that we are each to serve Jesus in all areas of life, including employment, wherever the Lord has placed us geographically and culturally, how can we encourage those called to vocational ministry to consider serving as a bi-vocational tentmaker?

Help Those Called to Serve

As we earnestly pray for the Lord to raise up more workers for the international harvest, and as we expect Him to answer those prayers, it is important that we journey alongside those whom God has specifically called to such ministry. May we pray, then, with expectancy and do our part to help people discern and learn as we invest in them along the way. And may we be diligent to present the vision and work of God's mission around the world to the generations that follow us as we pass to them the baton of ministry and leadership.

Principle in Practice

An Intentional Process

When part of a local church's DNA includes outreach and ministry outside the proverbial walls, where every ministry program has an element of being on mission and where many opportunities for ministry engagement are in place, you have a church that is committed to also raising up and sending out workers all over the world. Such is Cole Community Church, a large independent church in Boise, Idaho, that has a long, rich history in doing this very thing. Currently, Cole Community has twenty-one families who were sent from the church serving somewhere in the world, and several more are currently in the pipeline; the plan is to send out even more over the next decade.

Through a combination of prayer, challenging people, and training, this church has an intentional process in place to make it happen. This process comes naturally to this congregation, a church that is described as a "teaching church that is focused on discipleship" by Pastor Asher Sarjent, who oversees the global outreach ministries of the church. As people begin to sense what they feel is a call to serving the Lord cross-culturally, they begin a process of discernment where people like Pastor Sarjent meet with them to see if they meet, among other things, some established criteria for such ministry.

The next step is to then begin a mentoring relationship with an individual or couple who ideally has experience living abroad. This process also includes personalized, tailor-made training and involvement with ministry in the local community and at least once in another country. Cole happens to be a refugee resettlement city, so opportunities for cross-cultural ministry abound throughout their region. The length and depth of training depends on the individual and their personal and professional circumstances and how well they are progressing. This period also includes raising financial support for what will become their overseas ministry. When does the whole process begin? As early as childhood. In fact, the church even has a curriculum in place for fourth graders (the key age for decisions of faith and thoughts about the future) that is focused on global outreach. The curriculum is designed to share what the Bible teaches about evangelism and missions, how God has worked throughout history, and what our responsibility is as God's people in this world.

This investment in future missionaries is really a natural part of Cole Community's overall intent to equip "believers to become disciples of Jesus Christ who grow in loving God, loving others, and impacting the world," which is something that Pastor Sarjent suggests that "every church should be doing."

Raised Up and Sent

Red Village Church, led by Pastor Aaron Jozwiak, is a small Southern Baptist Church in Madison, Wisconsin, where missions has been part of the DNA from its beginning. "We are a missions-minded church," Jozwiak says. "We are committed to praying for missions, caring for missionaries related to our church, keeping people aware of the missional work in our city, region, and around the world, participating in cross-cultural ministry experiences, and investing in and recruiting people who will someday be missionaries themselves." Believing that it is the role of the local church to send out workers around the world, to date they have already raised up and personally sent out six missionaries from among them, always hoping and praying for even more.

What does this recruiting process look like for Red Village? The process begins where it should, with consistent prayer for more workers and missionaries to be identified, trained, and sent out among the peoples of the world to share the gospel message of Christ and His kingdom. As potential missionaries, often young adults in this church's case, are identified they enter into a coaching relationship with a seasoned Christ-follower and challenged to participate in local outreach efforts. They are also placed into ministry leadership roles, often as small group leaders, that help in their formation process.

This preparation period includes extensive in-house education as well, which is open for anyone in the church to be part of. These times of instruction are fondly called "Mission Labs" in which groups read books about missions, pray for missions, interact with active missionaries, and strategize about how to do missions locally, regionally, and globally. This kind of practical and educational experience especially, Jozwiak shares, has "become the greatest catalyst for the church to be more active in missions." Throughout this whole time of preparation, each future missionary is further connected with other missionaries, mission agencies, and mission boards to help them transition into long-term roles. Once sent, then, each missionary continues to be cared for by the church. The relationship doesn't end.

Suggested Resources

Todd Ahrend. *In This Generation: Looking to the Past to Reach the Present.* Colorado Springs: Book Villages, 2010.

Os Guinness. *The Call: Finding and Fulfilling the Central Purpose of Your Life.* Nashville: W Publishing Group, 1998.

Glenn Hanna. *Building Missionaries: Fostering Souls for Success on the Field.* Pittsburgh: Urban Press, 2018.

Gunter Krallman. *Mentoring for Mission.* Waynesboro, GA: Gabriel Publishing, 2002.

Patrick Lai. *Tentmaking: The Life and Work of Business as Missions.* Downers Grove: InterVarsity Press, 2005.

M. David Sills. *The Missionary Call: Find Your Place in God's Plan for the World.* Chicago: Moody Publishers, 2008.

David Wraight. *The Next Wave: Empowering the Generation That Will Change the World.* Colorado Springs: NavPress, 2007.

Notes

[1] Matthew 9:38-39 (NLT).

[2] David Wraight, *The Next Wave* (Colorado Springs: NavPress, 2007), xvii.

[3] See Mark 8:27-38, John 6:29, Romans 12:1-2, and 1 Peter 1:13-16.

[4] See Micah 6:8, Matthew 5:13-16, Acts 1:8, and 1 Peter 2:4-12.

[5] See Mark 12:28-34 and parallel passages.

[6] John Stott and Christopher J.H. Wright, *Christian Mission in the Modern World*, updated & expanded ed. (Downers Grove: InterVarsity Press, 2015), 31.

[7] Os Guinness, *The Call* (Nashville: W Publishing Group, 1998), 4.

[8] Again, John Stott says it well: "Jesus Christ calls all his disciples to "ministry," that is, to service...The only difference between us lies in the nature of the service we are called to render. Some are indeed called to be missionaries, evangelists or pastors, and others to the great professions of law, education, medicine and the social sciences. But others are called to commerce, to industry and farming, to accountancy and banking, to local government or parliament, and to the mass media, to homemaking and family building." (Stott and Wright, *Christian Mission*, 31.

[9] As missions pastor Glenn Hanna has written, "The goal is a healthy, growing, and self-aware candidate who is equipped for the battles that lie ahead." (Glenn Hanna, *Building Missionaries* (Pittsburgh: Urban Press, 2018), viii.

[10] For more insight into how Jesus and Paul invested in others in this way, see Appendix E.

[11] Patrick Lai, *Tentmaking* (Downers Grove: InterVarsity Press, 2005), 5-6.

ON MISSION TOGETHER

My hope and prayer as you read through this book is that not only are you more impassioned about being on mission for God, but that you and your congregation are also better equipped to more fully integrate missions into your ministry. Not as a single program, of course, but as part of everything we do as the Church. As you finish reading, I want to leave you with a few closing thoughts.

First, here is a reminder that this book has been focused on the global expression of the mission before us, however the same principles apply to some degree at local and regional expressions, too. As you engage on mission, then, remember to do so at each level and in all areas of life (missions is a life-style, after all)—personally, as a family, as a local church, and as the Church.

Second, I want to emphasize again that we are on mission *together* as God's people, not just as individuals. Evangelism and making disciples (locally, regionally, and globally) is a team sport. We're not meant to go solo. Each one of us has a part to play and contribution to make, no matter who we are, regardless of gender, age, ethnic background, socioeconomic status, level of education, or physical or mental capacity. So, as we live on mission together, it is important to know who God designed us to be as unique individuals who bring our personality, passions, skills and abilities, talents, preferences, and spiritual gifts to the table as we contribute to the overall mission of the Church and ministry to people.

Finally, please remember not to set the mission above God. As important as the mission is, when it's elevated to a level of idolatry, or if we start doing it our way in our own power, then we've gone too far. The scriptures are clear: we are to love God above all else and receive His love ourselves, then we love people in practical ways and reach out to them with the life-changing message of the gospel of Christ and His kingdom.

May the Lord richly bless you as you further integrate missions into your life and your church, engaging in mission together as the Church of Jesus Christ!

> *"Peace be with you! All authority in heaven and on earth has been given to Me [and] I am going to send you what My Father promised; receive the Holy Spirit.*
>
> *When the Holy Spirit comes on you, you will receive power, and you will be My witnesses in Jerusalem, and in all Judea and Samaria, and to the ends of the earth. This is what is written: The Messiah will suffer and rise from the dead on the third day, and repentance for the forgiveness of sins will be preached in His name to all nations, beginning at Jerusalem. You are witnesses of these things. Therefore, go into all the world and preach the gospel to all creation—and make disciples of all nations, baptizing them in the name of the Father and of the Son*

and of the Holy Spirit, and teaching them to obey every-thing I have commanded you. Whoever believes and is baptized will be saved, but whoever does not believe will be condemned.

And these signs will accompany those who believe: In My name they will drive out demons; they will speak in new tongues; they will pick up snakes with their hands; and when they drink deadly poison, it will not hurt them at all; they will place their hands on sick people, and they will get well. If you forgive the sins of anyone, their sins are forgiven; if you do not forgive them, they are not for-given. As the Father has sent Me, I am sending you—and surely, I am with you always, to the very end of the age."

- Matthew 28:18-20, Mark 16:15-18, Luke 24:46-49, John 20:21-23, Acts 1:8 -

APPENDIX A

MISSIONS MOBILIZATION TEAM

The ideal Missions Mobilization Team, in my opinion, consists of at least the following members:

- The **Team Leader** is the primary missions mobilizer for the church, providing key leadership and vision for cross-cultural ministry for the church. They oversee the work of the Team, serving as its main administrator.

- The **Secretary** takes official notes and provides them to MMT members and to appropriate church leadership and ministry committees.

- The **Missions Prayer Coordinator** leads and encourages missions prayer efforts by making prayer needs known to the church family, including special missionary prayer requests, cross-cultural ministry experiences, unreached people groups, international Christian relief work, and the persecuted Church.

- The **Missions Education Coordinator** develops and oversees venues for educational experiences regarding missions, so that the church knows what the Bible says about missions, what missions is, and what is happening with missionaries and various international ministries.

- The **Missions Experiences Coordinator** coordinates and oversees the church's local, regional, and global cross-cultural ministry experiences throughout the year.

- The **Teen Representative** acts as a liaison to, and creative voice from, teenagers in the church.

- The **Missionary Treasurer** provides financial insight and helps administer missions-related giving.

- If your church is part of a denomination that has them, then a **representative from women's and/or men's missions-focused organizations** should also be invited to part of the team.

- The **Senior Pastor** provides pastoral leadership and input.

Other positions may be added based on the church's desires and needs:

- The **Missions Conference Coordinator** is the primary leader for planning and overseeing missions conference(s) at the church. They could expand the role to be Missions Events Coordinator, serving to lead the planning and oversight of all missions awareness events at the church.

- The **Missions Promotion Coordinator** develops and oversees the promotion of missions awareness throughout church facilities and within church ministry programs.

- The **Missionary Care Coordinator** oversees various opportunities to express care for missionaries sent from or related to the church. For instance, they could keep in regular contact with missionaries, help the congregation to correspond with missionaries, hospitality ministries when a missionary is home.

- The **Cross-Cultural Ministry Partnerships Coordinator** manages ministry partnerships (local, regional, and global) between the church and missionaries/ fields/projects.

- The **International Student Ministry Coordinator** supervises the church's ministry to international students (foreign exchange students, students studying at local college or university) living and studying in the community.

- The **Immigrant Ministry Coordinator** administrates the church's ministry to immigrants living in the community.

- The **Refugee Ministry Coordinator** oversees the church's ministry to refugees living in the community.

- The **Adult Ministries Coordinator** (including Young Adult) provides input for adults in the church as it relates to educating and mobilizing them regarding cross-cultural ministry.

- The **Student Ministries Coordinator** or representative provides input for middle school, high school, and college students in the church as it relates to educating and mobilizing them regarding cross-cultural ministry.

- The **Children's Ministries Coordinator** or representative provides input for children in the church as it relates to educating and mobilizing them regarding cross-cultural ministry.

- The **Point-Person** from various ministries in the church (e.g., Sunday school or small groups) serves as liaisons to represented ministry as it relates to educating and mobilizing people regarding cross-cultural ministry.

- The **Cross-Cultural Ministry Recruitment Coordinator** oversees the recruitment of individuals for long-term, vocational involvement with cross-cultural ministry. They also help with short-term involvement.

- The **Cross-Cultural Ministry Training Coordinator** organizes the training and preparation of individuals for involvement with global short-term cross-cultural ministry experiences and/or ongoing local cross-cultural ministry efforts.

- The **Special Projects Coordinator** coordinates special missions-related projects. An example of this is Samaritan Purse's "Operation Christmas Child" project.

APPENDIX B

MISSIONS CONFERENCE IDEAS

Here are some conference activity ideas that have been tested and used by various churches that I have been part of or have interacted with:

- Match activities and opportunities with the missionaries' interests and abilities. Be creative (e.g. arrange for a missionary nurse or doctor to speak to the local medical professionals, have workers involved with marriage-related ministries speak about marriage to people from the church and the community, connect workers involved with relief ministries with various social service agencies in the community, etc.).

- Conduct a coloring and poster contest for the children (and youth)—displaying their work and giving awards to the best ones.

- Share meals together, international workers and congregation—breakfasts, lunches, dinners; international dinners work great, as do picnics, game dinners, and pig roasts.

- Have an ice cream social or a coffee house.

- Conduct a conference-long missions fair with material and representatives from various denominational, non-denominational, and parachurch missions ministries.

- Pray around the world, for missions efforts as well as peace and politics.

- Use children and youth in the worship services.

- Arrange for the missionaries to visit area schools— public and private, including colleges.

- Arrange for missionaries to speak at a community event at the local public library.

- Arrange for missionaries to speak to a local community civic organization group like the Lions Club or the Rotary Club (if the missionary is a member of one of these organizations, this is a great "in" with the community).

- Conduct youth events. Pizza parties or taco nights work well here.

- Have a bonfire.

- Conduct home meetings.

- Host a panel discussion with the missionaries.

- Have a family game night with the missionaries at the church.

- Conduct a separate missions conference for children and/or youth.

- Sponsor a 5K race and a 1K "family walk" for the purpose of raising missions awareness.

- Design a worship service that simulates worship from missionary's country.

- Work together with other churches—invite them to participate with you, plan joint congregational activities with the missionaries, etc.

- Conference Promotional Ideas

- Be creative and do it with excellence.

- Decorate the church with missions and intercultural items, including display tables for missionary items or church missions trip curios.

- Display flags from around the world, at least the countries where your church-affiliated (or denominational) missionaries work. At the very least, this could work with the flags from your conference missionaries.

- If part of a denomination, display the denominational missions conference posters (perhaps even year-round) and make use of the promotional materials that are produced by the denomination and made available to your church.

- Use age-appropriate advertising for all ages in the church.

- Use the worship service bulletin, church newsletter, and church website for announcements regarding the conference as well as trivia information regarding the missionary and place(s) where they serve in ministry.

- Have the pastor personally invite members of the congregation to participate and pray for the conference.

- Advertise in the local newspaper, the local radio and TV stations, and on social networking sites such as Facebook, Instagram, and Twitter.

- Place lawn signs advertising the event in front of the church (and at people's homes).

- Make use of drama or other creative means of announcing the conference in the worship services.

- Have missionaries record (audio or video) a personal greeting for the church and play that greeting prior to the conference and their arrival.

- If part of a denomination, some other helpful information may be available through your national office and/or website.

RESPONDING TO THE PERSECUTED CHURCH

Here are some ways that we can be aware of and respond to our brothers and sisters in Christ around the world who daily suffer for following Jesus.

1. Passion
   - Develop a passion for God and for serving Him.

   - Develop a passion for God's work, which is global in nature; God's heart should be our heart.

2. Process
   - Be informed, know and process what the Bible says about persecution for the sake of God and His kingdom (in both the Old and New Testaments). See Matthew 5:10-12 & 43-48, Matthew 10:16-23, John 15:18-23, Acts 12:1-17, Hebrews 13:3, and 1 Peter 4:12-19.

   - Be informed about what is happening around the world regarding persecution, and then inform others; read and listen to the news, pay attention to current events, connect with organizations like Open Doors International, International Christian Concern, and Voice of the Martyrs.

3. Persuade / Protest
   - Stand up and speak for those who cannot stand or speak for themselves.

   - Write letters to government officials in behalf of those suffering, help enact legislation, etc.

4. Provide
   - Donate money and materials to organizations and ministries that are actively engaged in ministry to the persecuted church.

   - Provide encouragement to those suffering by writing letters to them and even personally visiting them if possible.

5. Pray
   - God moves when we pray. Implore the King of Heaven to take action.

   - This is something anyone can (and should) do, regardless of age, place, or circumstance.

   - Pray for protection and courage for the persecuted, for the persecutors, for Christ's Church to grow and God's kingdom to be recognized, for biblical literacy and theological education and training, for international and local church workers (guidance, protection, needs), for open doors to remain open and closed doors to open, and for peace

SHORT-TERM MISSIONS EXPERIENCES

As mentioned in Chapter 7, there are some important issues concerning short-term missions experiences that should be addressed, namely, (1) the tension of process versus project, (2) the benefits and drawbacks of short-term missions experiences, and (3) the impact of short-term missions experiences on long-term missions involvement. Each of these items will be addressed here.

Process vs. Project

Millennials and Generation Z are generally attracted to focused, shorter-term *projects* and to being personally involved with other cultures via hands-on activities and cross-cultural friendships. In terms of missions, they prefer to "taste and see" missions trips for the short-term before committing to the long-term. This is not surprising considering that these generations sometimes shy away from anything long-term, especially particular career commitments. Western culture contributes to this mindset by bringing certain expectations upon them to move ahead and be fresh, relevant, and cutting-edge.

Historically, though, missions strategy has typically been developed in terms of having a long-term, incarnational approach where the missionary goes to live among people to develop relationships and do relational ministry. This is a *process* that takes time, with many years of hard work that involves sacrifice, faith, a commitment to people of other cultures, and a commitment to learning their language and customs. It requires people with missiological skills who will stay long enough to establish friendships, reach the lost, and plant churches.

Obviously, a tension exists between these two approaches, but they are not in conflict. Defenders of "process" argue that long-term worker commitment cannot be replaced with short-term spurts of service. However, the Bible does not speak in terms of a lifetime calling to one place. Rather, it speaks of a lifetime commitment to obedience, doing whatever the Lord wants whenever and wherever He desires. In essence, people should be able to make use of new and creative ways of doing missions while they seek to serve the Lord by making disciples throughout the world.

For project-minded people, shorter-term agreements can also be made and renewed. This would allow for opportunity for one to serve the Lord obediently in a potential variety of ways wherever He chooses.

While vocational workers are preferred, short-term international workers are certainly needed and will continue to contribute to the task of world evangelization. The tension between process and project cannot be ignored; it will always be there. Therefore, the balance of taking a "both-and" approach is needed.

Benefits and Drawbacks

Short-term missions experiences are valuable and needed. While long-term, incarnational commitment is necessary for healthy and lasting cross-cultural ministry to occur, short-term ministry teams play a significant role in accomplishing God's plan in the region and in the life of the participant. Again, perhaps a "both-and" approach is needed, where both sides learn from each other and ministry insights are gained by all. Such an approach would prioritize the national church and its needs, with vocational workers working alongside national church leaders to develop a long-term strategy for evangelization and church planting.

Short-term missions experiences could be coordinated with the resident missionaries in a way that contributes to the long-term strategy rather than interrupting it. Here is where ministry partnerships come in as they can be established between local churches in the United States and a particular missionary or missionary family, missions project or mission field (or even long-term involvement with a national church); part of the partnership would include a series of short-term experiences with participants from the churches that are involved.

The hopeful benefits of short-term missions experiences include the following:

- Participants are given exposure to missions and missionaries in a cross-cultural setting.

- Participants gain some hands-on ministry training and experience in a cross-cultural setting.

- Global vision is stimulated as people see God at work around the world, creating a new or renewed interest in missions and probable long-term missions involvement.

- Prayer for missions is personalized and contextualized.

- Giving to missions is increased.

- Certain tasks or projects can be done that otherwise could not be done (e.g. medical missions, veterinary care, some types of construction, etc.).

- Some of the work of the international workers (and the national church) can be made easier and more productive, especially when specialized short-term teams are able to finish specific projects.

- Long-term vocational workers are often mobilized and recruited as a result of short-term involvement.

Of course, short-term missions also has its drawbacks, including the following:

- The importance of short-term experiences is often overstated in terms of missions strategy.

- The experiences are too short and too limited. There is not enough time for authentic exposure to the mission field (with all its ups and downs) or to the missionary and what they do, time for effective ministry is limited, and nationals sometimes do not take short-termers seriously.

- Participants often fail to understand culture and customs properly, resulting in cross-cultural insensitivity and ineffective ministry.

- Ministry results are limited.

- Short-term trips are often too expensive and sometimes take money and resources away from long-term missionary and national church ministry efforts.

- Missionaries can be overloaded, interrupted, distracted, inconvenienced, and interfered with.

- National church ministries can be ignored or overwhelmed.

- Participants can have the wrong motivations for taking part in short-term mission teams, wanting to build their resumes, be religious tourists, or become self-proclaimed missions experts.

Long-Term Missions Involvement

The impact of short-term missions experiences on ongoing missions involvement is significant. As noted above, some of the benefits of being involved with missions via a short-term project are increased awareness of, praying for, and giving to the work of world evangelization and disciple making.[1] It was also pointed out that such short-term involvement can be an effective means of mobilizing and recruiting long-term vocational missionaries.

Many missionaries testify that their "call" to the mission field was discerned during their participation on a short-term missions team; missions agencies and denominations frequently report that many of their personnel who have committed to being long-term missionaries first had at least one short-term missions experience.[2] It appears, then, that at one level involvement on a short-term basis may help lay a critical foundation for missions awareness and involvement while generating at least openness to serving as a missionary for life.

Indeed, short-term missions experiences are often the place where long-term decisions are made.

Conclusion

This brief exploration of three significant issues reveals that long-term, vocational missionaries are preferred over short-term missionaries. However, short-term missionaries are definitely needed, and they will continue to contribute to the task of world evangelization. As mentioned in Chapter 7, local churches and ministries can help their people in this area of cross-cultural ministry experience primarily by offering short-term missions opportunities that are done with excellence and with clear intentions of doing ministry with long-term mission field strategy in mind.

Notes

[1] It should be noted, though, that more research has been done in this area, indicating that these benefits may not be as significant as once thought. See the series of articles in *Christianity Today* in 2005 that summarized these findings—http://www.christianitytoday.com/ct/2005/juneweb-only/12.0c.html. Short-term missions experiences, with both their benefits and drawbacks, have since been studied even further and more extensively written about. Consult the resources noted at the end of this book for more information and critique.

[2] STEM Ministries discovered in their 1999 study of the effectiveness of short-term missions that such experiences are often the most important influence for people who decide to serve long-term as missionaries. (Daniel P. McDonough and Roger P. Peterson, *Can Short-Term Missions Really Create Long-Term Career Missionaries?* (Minneapolis: STEM Ministries, 1999), 10.

JESUS & PAUL ON INVESTING IN OTHERS

As mentioned in Chapter 9, both Jesus and the Apostle Paul give us great insight into recruiting people to ministry and investing in them in powerful ways. Here, more specifically, are some insights to glean from.

Jesus

Jesus' method of recruiting people to ministry was focused around building relationships with people. He loved and served everybody, but He also devoted a large part of His ministry to 12 men who became known as the apostles. The gospels of Mark and Luke record that after spending significant time in prayer, Jesus recruited this core group of disciples to be *apostle-apprentices* who would spend a majority, if not all, of their time with Him, observing and participating in His life and ministry.[1]

In fact, Jesus spent the bulk of His time training these men who enthusiastically left careers and normal life behind to follow Him.[2] He became their mentor; they became His apprentices. His focus here was simply to be with them, teaching them and building their character so that they would eventually extend His ministry around the world. A.B. Bruce noted in his classic work *The Training of the Twelve*,

> There were to be students of Christian doctrine, and occasional fellow-laborers in the work of the kingdom, and eventually Christ's chosen trained agents for propagating the faith after He Himself had left the earth. From the time of their being chosen, indeed, the twelve entered on a regular apprenticeship for the great office of apostleship, in the course of which they were to learn, in the privacy of an intimate daily fellowship with their Master, what they should be, do, believe, and teach, as His witnesses and ambassadors to the world. Henceforth the training of these men was to be a constant and prominent part of Christ's personal work.[3]

Missionary Gunter Krallmann puts it this way:

> Through the disciples' continual exposure to who he was, what he did and said, Jesus intended them to discern and absorb his vision, mindset and mode of operation. He desired them to become so saturated with the influences arising from his example and teaching, his attitudes, actions and anointing, that every single area of their lives would be impacted towards greater likeness to himself. The approach he decided on was simple and informal, practical and wholistic. The totality of shared life experiences made up the disciples' classroom, and their teacher's words merely needed to further elucidate the lessons already gained from his life.[4]

An important dynamic of this apprenticeship model was that Jesus included (as alluded to in Bruce's and Krallmann's comments above) these men, along with other disciples, on ministry trips and ministry occasions. He invited them to observe and participate in all the aspects of His ministry so that they may learn firsthand how the Master did it. This is seen clearly in several passages: (1) In Matthew 4:23-25 it can be assumed that Jesus' disciples were with Him in Galilee as He taught, preached, and healed people; (2) Mark 1:21-28 notes that they were with Him in Capernaum as He taught people and delivered at least one man from demonic possession; (3) Matthew 8:14-17/Mark 1:29-39/Luke 4:38-44 record their presence with Jesus at Simon Peter's home, where they observed Him healing people, preaching the gospel, and casting out demons; (4) Luke reports in Luke 8:1-3 that the apostles, along with other disciples, were with Jesus as He went from one city and village to another "proclaiming the good news of the kingdom of God" (NIV); and (5) Two other times Mark (3:7-12, 9:30ff) mentions that Jesus' disciples were alone with Him in Galilee before crowds of people pressed in upon them.

These men not only spent significant time with Jesus, studying and sharing in His life and ministry, but they were also *sent* by Jesus *to serve* and to represent Him. The Gospels of Matthew, Mark, and Luke all give a clear account of a time when Jesus sent His apostles out in pairs among the cities and villages to do what He Himself had been doing—the very things they had seen and been involved with.[5] Having been given the authority of Jesus, these "apprentice missionaries"[6] were charged with preaching a message of repentance and the kingdom of God/heaven, healing the sick, cleansing lepers, driving out demons, and raising the dead—all things that they had personally seen Jesus do. The instructions beyond this were simple: totally depend on God to provide

everything, expect opposition, and give of themselves to serving others for the sake of following and serving Jesus. By all
accounts they were successful.

Luke records a related occasion when Jesus sent out seventy of His followers, again in pairs, ahead of Him to various cities that He would be visiting and ministering in.[7] As
with the apostles, these disciples were sent into God's harvest
field (verse 2) to preach the nearness of God's kingdom (in
Jesus), heal the sick, and cast out demons as representatives of
Jesus. They also had the same instructions—fully rely on God
and expect opposition. They too were successful, reporting
to Jesus all that they had seen and experienced. This passage
further indicates that Jesus spent some time debriefing these
ministers of the gospel.[8]

When considering what Jesus did, then, in terms of investing in people and recruiting them for ministry, we can remember the twelve appointed apostle-apprentices. Jesus was
their master and mentor who taught them how to live and
how to do ministry—empowered by and dependent upon
God while living selfless lives of sacrifice and love. He was
both their teacher and their friend, guiding them each step of
the way and gently (and at times not so gently) nudging them
into doing ministry on their own (humanly speaking). They
were Jesus' ministry team—people that He personally called
and heavily invested in to duplicate His approach to ministry
and in turn change the world.

Paul

Just as Jesus provided on-the-job training for His disciples
so Paul took people alongside himself to show them not just
how to live, but also how to love and serve others. He, too,
invested his life in certain individuals, taking them along on
his missionary journeys and having them assist him in the

various parts of his ministry. Included among these ministry assistants (and leaders) were Luke (Acts 1:1, Col. 4:14, 2 Tim. 4:11, Philem. 1:23), John Mark (Acts 12:25, 13:5; cf. Philem. 1:24), Silas (Acts 15:22, 27, 40), Timothy (Acts 16:1-3, 20:4), Priscilla and Aquila (Acts 18:18-19, Rom. 16:3; cf. 1 Cor. 16:19), Gaius (Acts 19:29, 20:4), Aristarchus (Acts 19:29, 20:4; cf. Acts 27:2, Col. 4:10, Philem. 1:24), Sopater of Berea (Acts 20:4), Secundus (Acts 20:4), Tychicus (Acts 20:4; cf. Eph. 6:21, Col. 4:7-9, 2 Tim. 4:12), Trophimus (Acts 20:4; cf. 2 Tim. 4:20), Epaphroditus (Phil. 2:25-30), and Epaphras (Col. 4:12-13; cf. Philem. 1:23). These were all people that Paul brought into his life for them to observe how he did ministry and led the Church so that they also, with Paul's blessing and authority, would be able to do ministry (even cross-culturally) and provide leadership to congregations.

Paul also had at least two men who became his *apprentices*—Timothy and Titus, who ministered together with Paul as his close associates and whom Paul confidently sent to places to handle difficult situations. Timothy accompanied Paul on his second and third missionary journeys, as well as various other places of ministry.[9] Paul, Scripture records, saw him not only as a fellow worker or ministry assistant,[10] but also as a spiritual son.[11] Timothy coauthored letters to churches with Paul[12] and was sent by Paul, with his authority, to some churches to provide leadership and instruction.[13] So close was their relationship that there are even two letters written to Timothy that are included in the canon of Scripture, letters in which Paul reminds and instructs Timothy about how to live and minister as he passed on to him the baton of leadership.

The other person that Paul mentored was Titus, who was a partner and fellow worker[14] of Paul's who went with him to, among other places, Jerusalem to meet with the

other apostles.[15] Along with Timothy, Titus was also considered by Paul to be his "true child in a common faith"[16]
and a "brother."[17] Titus, it is known, was also sent to some
churches[18] and was instructed, as Timothy was, by Paul in a
letter about how to do ministry.[19] Titus eventually went on a
missionary journey of his own, going to Dalmatia.[20]

The apostle Paul, then, continued Jesus' pattern of teaching and preaching the gospel of God's kingdom to all people,
sharing his life with individuals while recruiting (and mobilizing) them for ministry (both domestic and cross-cultural)
as a friend and mentor.

Now imagine what it would look like if we invested
our lives in others in the same ways that Jesus and Paul did.
Among other things, we have models here to learn from and
principles to make use of as we pour ourselves into others for
the sake of the gospel and the glory of God throughout the
world.

Notes

[1] Mark 3:13-19 and Luke 6:12-16.

[2] See page 30 of A.B. Bruce, *The Training of the Twelve* (1894; reprint, Grand Rapids: Kregel Publications, 1971) and page 97 of Andreas J. Kostenberger and Peter T. O'Brien, *Salvation to the Ends of the Earth: A Biblical Theology of Mission* (Downers Grove: InterVarsity Press, 2001).

[3] Bruce, *The Training of the Twelve*, 30.

[4] Gunter Krallmann, *Mentoring for Mission* (Waynesboro, GA: Gabriel Publishing, 2002), 53.

[5] Matthew 10:1-42, Mark 6:7-13, and Luke 9:1-11.

[6] Bruce, *The Training of the Twelve*, 100.

[7] Luke 10:1-24. Important to note here is the move to involve more than just the twelve apostles with the task; everyone was to represent Jesus and speak for Him.

[8] It can be safely assumed that Jesus also helped His twelve apostle-apprentices to process this ministry experience as well.

[9] See Acts 16:1-3, 18:5, and 20:4.

[10] See Romans 16:21 and 2 Corinthians 1:19.

[11] Philippians 2:22, 1 Timothy 1:2, 18, and 2 Timothy 1:2. William Mounce points out that this carries with it Paul's authority as an apostle to deal with Church and ministry matters; Timothy speaks with Paul's authority. (William D. Mounce, *Word Biblical Commentary: Pastoral Epistles* (Nashville: Thomas Nelson Publishers, 2000), 7)

[12] 2 Corinthians 1:1, Philippians 1:1, Colossians 1:1, 1 Thessalonians 1:1, 2 Thessalonians 1:1, and Philemon 1:1.

[13] Acts 19:22, 1 Corinthians 4:17, 16:10-11, 1 Thessalonians 3:2-3, 6, and Philippians 2:19-24.

[14] 2 Corinthians 8:23; cf. 2 Corinthians 7:5-7 and 13-16.

[15]Galatians 2:1-5.

[16]Titus 1:4. Titus, as well as Timothy, was invested with Paul's apostolic authority. (Mounce, *Pastoral Epistles*, 382)

[17]2 Corinthians 2:13.

[18]2 Corinthians 8:6-7, 16-24, 12:18.

[19]Note Titus 2:1 and 3:1.

[20]2 Timothy 4:10.

APPENDIX F

ON MISSION
TOGETHER: RESOURCES

The *Missio Dei* and Missional Living

Bruce Riley Ashford, ed. *Theology and Practice of Mission: God, the Church, and the Nations.* Nashville: B&H Academic, 2011.

David J. Bosch. *Transforming Mission: Paradigm Shifts in Theology of Mission.* Maryknoll, NY: Orbis Books, 1991.

Michael W. Goheen. *A Light to the Nations: The Missional Church and the Biblical Story.* Grand Rapids: Baker Academic, 2011.

Darrell L. Guder, ed. *Missional Church: A Vision for the Sending of the Church in North America.* Grand Rapids: Wm.B. Eerdmans Publishing Co., 1998.

Reggie McNeal. *Missional Renaissance: Changing the Scorecard for the Church.* San Francisco: Jossey-Bass, 2009.

Alan J. Roxburgh and M. Scott Boren. *Introducing the Missional Church: What It Is, Why It Matters, How to Become One.* Grand Rapids: Baker Books, 2009.

Denny Spitters and Matthew Ellison. *When Everything is*

Missions. Orlando: BottomLine Media, 2017.

John Stott and Christopher J.H. Wright. *Christian Mission in the Modern World*, updated and expanded ed. Downers Grove: InterVarsity Press, 2015.

Charles Van Engen. *God's Missionary People: Rethinking the Purpose of the Local Church*. Grand Rapids: Baker Book House, 1991.

Christopher J.H. Wright. *The Mission of God's People: A Biblical Theology of the Church's Mission*. Grand Rapids: Zondervan, 2010.

Biblical-Theological Basis for Missions

Roland Allen. *Missionary Methods: St. Paul's or Ours?* rep. Grand Rapids: Wm.B. Eerdmans Publishing Company, 2002.

Bruce Riley Ashford, ed. *Theology and Practice of Mission: God, the Church, and the Nations*. Nashville: B&H Academic, 2011.

Mike Barnett, ed. *Discovering the Mission of God: Best Missional Practices for the 21st Century*. Downers Grove: IVP Academic, 2012.

David J. Bosch. *Transforming Mission: Paradigm Shifts in Theology of Mission*. Maryknoll, NY: Orbis Books, 1991.

Kevin DeYoung and Greg Gilbert. *What is the Mission of the Church? Making Sense of Social Justice, Shalom, and the Great Commission*. Wheaton: Crossway, 2011.

Michael W. Goheen. *A Light to the Nations: The Missional Church and the Biblical Story*. Grand Rapids: Baker Academic, 2011.

Walter C. Kaiser, Jr. *Mission in the Old Testament: Israel as a Light to the Nations*. Grand Rapids: Baker Books, 2000.

Andreas J. Kostenberger and Peter T. O'Brien. *Salvation to the Ends of the Earth: A Biblical Theology of Mission*. Downers Grove: InterVarsity Press, 2001.

William J. Larkin, Jr. and Joel F. Williams, eds. *Mission in the*

New Testament: An Evangelical Approach. Maryknoll, NY: Orbis Books, 1998.

Lesslie Newbigin. *The Open Secret: An Introduction to the Theology of Mission.* rev. ed. Grand Rapids: Wm.B. Eerdmans Publishing Co., 1995.

Craig Ott et al. *Encountering Theology of Mission: Biblical Foundations, Historical Developments, and Contemporary Issues.* Grand Rapids: Baker Academic, 2010.

C. Rene Padilla. *Mission Between the Times.* Grand Rapids: Wm.B. Eerdmans Publishing Company, 1985.

John Piper. *Let the Nations Be Glad!: The Supremacy of God in Missions,* 2nd ed. Grand Rapids: Baker Books, 2003.

Vinay Samuel and Chris Sugden, eds. *Mission as Transformation: A Theology of the Whole Gospel.* Oxford: Regnum Books International, 1999.

John Stott, ed. *Making Christ Known: Historic Mission Documents from the Lausanne Movement, 1974-1989.* Grand Rapids: Wm.B. Eerdman's Publishing Company, 1996.

John Stott and Christopher J.H. Wright. *Christian Mission in the Modern World.* updated and expanded ed. Downers Grove: IVP Books, 2015.

William D. Taylor, ed. *Global Missiology For the 21st Century: The Iguassu Dialogue.* Grand Rapids: Baker Academic, 2000.

Timothy C. Tennent. *Invitation to World Missions: A Trinitarian Missiology for the Twenty-first Century.* Grand Rapids: Kregel Publications, 2010.

Charles Van Engen. *God's Missionary People: Rethinking the Purpose of the Local Church.* Grand Rapids: Baker Book House, 1991.

Ralph D. Winter and Steven C. Hawthorne, eds. *Perspectives on the World Christian Movement: A Reader.* 4th ed. Pasadena: William Carey Library, 2009. (Part One)

Christopher J.H. Wright. *The Mission of God: Unlocking the Bible's*

Grand Narrative. Downers Grove: IVP Academic, 2006.
Christopher J.H. Wright. *The Mission of God's People: A Biblical Theology of the Church's Mission*. Grand Rapids: Zondervan, 2010.

History of Missions

Mike Barnett, ed. *Discovering the Mission of God: Best Missional Practices for the 21st Century*. Downers Grove: IVP Academic, 2012. (Part Two)

Stephen Neill. *A History of Christian Missions*, 2nd ed. London: Penguin Books, 1986.

Eckhard J. Schabel. *Early Christian Mission*. 2 vols. Downers Grove: IVP Academic, 2004.

Robert J. Stevens and Brian Johnson, eds. *Profiles of African-American Missionaries*. Pasadena: William Carey Library, 2012.

Ruth A. Tucker. *From Jerusalem to Irian Jaya: A Biographical History of Christian Missions*, 2nd ed. Grand Rapids: Zondervan, 2004.

Andrew Walls. *The Missionary Movement in Christian History: Studies in the Transmission of Faith*. Maryknoll, NY: Orbis Books, 1996.

Ralph D. Winter and Steven C. Hawthorne, eds. *Perspectives on the World Christian Movement: A Reader*. 4th ed. Pasadena: William Carey Library, 2009. (Part Two)

Missionary Biographies

Missions Awareness & Education

Paul Borthwick. *A Mind for Missions: 10 Ways to Build Your World Vision*. Colorado Springs: Navpress, 1987.

Paul Borthwick. *Great Commission Great Compassion: Following Jesus and Loving the World*. Downers Grove: IVP Books, 2015.

Paul Borthwick. *How to Be a World-Class Christian: Becoming*

Part of God's Global Kingdom. 2nd ed. Downers Grove: InterVarsity Press, 2009.

Paul Borthwick. *Western Christians in Global Mission: What's the Role of the North American Church?* Downers Grove: InterVarsity Press, 2012.

Paul Borthwick. *Youth and Missions: Expanding Your Students' Worldview.* 2nd ed. Waynesboro, GA: OM Literature, 1998.

David Bryant. *In the Gap: What It Means to Be A World Christian.* Ventura, CA: Regal Books, 1984.

Paul-Gordon Chandler. *God's Global Mosaic: What We Can Learn from Christians Around the World.* Downers Grove: InterVarsity Press, 2000.

Dan & Dave Davidson and George Verwer. *God's Great Ambition.* Waynesboro, GA: Gabriel Publishing, 2001.

Ann Dunagan. *The Mission Minded Child: Raising a New Generation to Fulfill God's Purpose.* Colorado Springs: Authentic Publishing, 2007.

Carl F. Ellis, Jr. *Going Global Beyond the Boundaries: The Role of the Black Church in the Great Commission of Jesus Christ.* Chicago: Urban Ministries, Inc., 2005.

Frontier Ventures. *Perspectives on the World Christian Movement* course (information at www.frontierventures.org/ministries/perspectives)

Graham Hill. *GlobalChurch: Reshaping Our Conversations, Renewing Our Mission, Revitalizing Our Churches.* Downers Grove: InterVarsity Press, 2016.

David Horner. *When Missions Shape the Mission: You and Your Church Can Reach the World.* Nashville: B&H Publishing Group, 2011.

Philip Jenkins. *The Next Christendom: The Coming of Global Christianity.* 3rd ed. New York: Oxford University Press, 2011.

Andy Johnson. *Missions: How the Local Church Goes Global.*
Wheaton: Crossway, 2017.

Leonidas A. Johnson. *The African-American Church: Waking Up to God's Missionary Call.* Pasadena: William Carey Library, 2006.

Patrick Johnstone. *The Church is Bigger Than You Think: The Unfinished Work of World Evangelization.* Pasadena: William Carey Library, 1998.

David Mays. *Becoming a World-Changing Church.* 2010. (available at http://davidmays.org/Becoming.pdf)

George Miley. *Loving the Church...Blessing the Nations: Pursuing the Role of Local Churches in Global Mission.* Waynesboro, GA: Authentic Books, 2003.

Andrew Murray. *Key to the Missionary Problem.* rep. Ft. Washington, PA: Christian Literature Crusade, 1979.

Ross Paterson. *The Antioch Factor: The Hidden Message of the Book of Acts.* Kent, England: Sovereign World, 2000.

David Platt. *Radical: Taking Back Your Faith from the American Dream.* Colorado Springs: Multnomah Books, 2010.

Jim and Judy Raymo. *Millennials and Missions: A Generation Faces a Global Challenge.* Pasadena: William Carey Library, 2014.

David Shibley. *The Missions Addiction: Capturing God's Passion for the World.* Lake Mary, FL: Charisma House, 2001.

Bob Sjogren and Bill & Amy Stearns. *Run with the Vision: A Remarkable Global Plan for the 21st Century Church.* Minneapolis: Bethany House Publishers, 1995.

Bill & Amy Stearns. *2020 Vision: Amazing Stories of What God is Doing Around the World.* Minneapolis: Bethany House, 2005.

Richard Tiplady, ed. *Postmission: World Mission by a Postmodern Generation.* Carlisle, Cumbria, UK: Paternoster Press, 2002.

Vaughn J. Walston and Robert J. Stevens, eds. *African-American Experience in World Mission: A Call Beyond Community.* 2nd ed. Pasadena: William Carey Library, 2009.

David and Lorene Wilson, eds. *Pipeline: Engaging the Church in Missionary Mobilization.* Littleton: William Carey Press, 2018.
Ralph D. Winter and Steven C. Hawthorne, eds. *Perspectives on the World Christian Movement: A Reader.* 4th ed. Pasadena: William Carey Library, 2009.
David Wraight. *The Next Wave: Empowering the Generation That Will Change Our World.* Colorado Springs: Navpress, 2007.

Missions Mobilization Leadership

Catalyst Services, "Leaders Toolbox" (available at http://catalystservices.org/leaders-toolbox/)
Global Focus. *Growing a Great Commission Church* seminar (information at www.GlobalFocus.info)
James F. Engel and William A. Dyrness. *Changing the Mind of Missions: Where Have We Gone Wrong?* Downers Grove: InterVarsity Press, 2000.
David Mays. *Stuff You Need to Know About Missions in Your Church, Vols. 1-5.* (information & availability at http://davidmays.org/Resources/resmays.html)
David Mays. *Becoming a World-Changing Church.* 2010. (available at http://davidmays.org/Becoming.pdf)
David Mays. *The Mission Leadership Team: Mobilizing Your Church to Touch the World.* Stone Mountain, GA: The Mission Exchange, 2010.
Steve Moore. *While You Were Micro-Sleeping: Fresh Insights on the Changing Face of North American Missions.* Stone Mountain, GA: The Mission Exchange, 2009.

Praying for Missions

Jason Mandryk. *Operation World: The Definitive Prayer Guide to Every Nation* (7th ed.). Colorado Springs: Biblica, 2010.

Jason Mandryk. *Pray for the World: A New Prayer Resource from Operation World*. Downers Grove: InterVarsity Press, 2015.

Molly Wall and Jason Mandryk, eds. *Window on the World: An Operation World Prayer Resource*. rev. ed. Downers Grove: InterVarsity Press, 2018. (kid's version of *Operation World*)

Kids Praying for Kids DVD (resource for encouraging and teaching children to be intercessors for missions; available at http://www.prayershop.org/Kids-Praying-for-Kids-DVD-p/chi-rei-dv-001.htm)

Websites: www.globalprayerdigest.org, joshuaproject.net/pray, www.operationworld.org

Giving to Missions

Randy Alcorn. *Money, Possessions, and Eternity*. rev. ed. Wheaton: Tyndale House Publishers, Inc., 2003.

Randy Alcorn. *The Treasure Principle: Unlocking the Secret of Joyful Giving*. rev. ed. Colorado Springs: Multnomah, 2017.

Craig L. Blomberg. *Christians in an Age of Wealth: A Biblical Theology of Stewardship*. Grand Rapids: Zondervan, 2013.

Jonathan J. Bonk. *Missions and Money: Affluence as a Western Missionary Problem*. Maryknoll, NY: Orbis Books, 1991.

Kennon L. Callahan. *Giving and Stewardship in an Effective Church: A Guide for Every Member*. San Francisco: Jossey-Bass Publishers, 1992.

Steve Corbett and Brian Fikkert. *When Helping Hurts: How to Alleviate Poverty without Hurting the Poor...and Yourself*. 2nd ed. Chicago: Moody Press, 2012.

Gilles Gravelle. *The Age of Global Giving: A Practical Guide for Donors and Funding Recipients for Our Time*. Pasadena: William Carey Library, 2014.

Robert D. Lupton. *Toxic Charity: How Churches and Charities Hurt Those They Help, and How to Reverse It*. New York:

HarperOne, 2011.

Arif Mohamed, Brett Elder, and Stephen Grabill, eds. *Kingdom Stewardship: Occasional Papers Presented by the Lausanne Resource Mobilization Working Group for Cape Town 2010*. Grand Rapids: Christian's Library Press, 2010.

Tom Nelson. *The Economics of Neighborly Love: Investing in Your Community's Compassion and Capacity*. Downers Grove: InterVarsity Press, 2017.

Michael Rhodes, Robby Holt, and Brian Fikkert. *Practicing the King's Economy: Honoring Jesus in How We Work, Earn, Spend, Save, and Give*. Grand Rapids: Baker Books, 2018.

Eugene C. Roehlkepartain, Elanah Dalyah Naftali, and Laura Musegades. *Growing Up Generous: Engaging Youth in Giving and Serving*. Bethesda: The Alban Institute, 2000.

Ronald J. Sider. *Rich Christians in An Age of Hunger: Moving from Affluence to Generosity*. 6th ed. Nashville: Thomas Nelson, 2015.

Chris Willard and James E. Sheppard. *Contagious Generosity: Creating a Culture of Giving in Your Church*. Grand Rapids: Zondervan, 2012.

Sending & Caring for Missionaries

Betty Barnett. *Friend Raising: Building a Missionary Support Team That Lasts*. Seattle: YWAM Publishing, 1991.

Steve Beirn with George W. Murray. *Well Sent: Reimagining the Church's Missionary-Sending Process*. Ft. Washington, PA: CLC Publications, 2015.

Pam Echerd and Alice Arathoon, eds. *Understanding and Nurturing the Missionary Family*. Pasadena: William Carey Library, 1989.

Glenn Hanna. *Building Missionaries: Fostering Souls for Success on the Field*. Pittsburgh: Urban Press, 2018.

Dr. David Harley. *Preparing to Serve: Training for*

Cross-Cultural Mission. Pasadena: William Carey Library, 1995.

Steve Hoke and Bill Taylor. *Global Mission Handbook: A Guide for Crosscultural Service*. rev. ed. Downers Grove: InterVarsity Press, 2009.

Peter Jordan. *Re-Entry: Making the Transition from Missions to Life at Home*. Seattle: YWAM Publishers, 1992.

John McVay, gen. ed. *Ask a Missionary: Time-Tested Answers from Those Who've Been There*. Colorado Springs: Authentic Publishing, 2010.

Kelly O'Donnell, ed. *Doing Member Care Well: Perspectives and Practices from Around the World*. Pasadena: William Carey Library, 2002.

Neal Pirolo. *Serving as Senders Today*. rev. & exp. San Diego: Emmaus Road International, Inc., 2012.

Neal Pirolo. *The Reentry Team: Caring for Your Returning Missionaries*. San Diego: Emmaus Road International, 2000.

David C. Pollock and Ruth E. VanReken. *Third Culture Kids*. rev. ed. Boston: Nicholas Brealey Publishing, 2009.

Brian Rust and Barry McLeish. *The Support-Raising Handbook: A Guide for Christian Workers*. Downers Grove: InterVarsity Press, 1984.

Steve Shadrach. *The God Ask: A Fresh, Biblical Approach to Personal Support Raising*. Fayetteville: CMM Press, 2013.

Ryan Shaw. *Spiritual Equipping for Mission: Thriving as God's Message Bearers*. Downers Grove: InterVarsity Press, 2014.

Pete Sommer. *Getting Sent: A Relational Approach to Support Raising*. Downers Grove: InterVarsity Press, 1999.

Joel Sutton, ed. *Whom Shall We Send? Understanding the Essentials of Sending Missionaries*. Self-Published, CreateSpace, 2016.

Trinity Church Missionary Care Team. *Mind the Gaps:*

Engaging the Church in Missionary Care. Kansas City, MO: Mind the Gaps, 2015.

Mabel Williamson. *Have We No Rights? A Frank Discussion of the "Rights" of Missionaries*. Self-published, Create Space, 2010.

David and Lorene Wilson, eds. *Pipeline: Engaging the Church in Missionary Mobilization*. Littleton: William Carey Press, 2018.

Marsha Woodard. *To Timbuktu & Beyond: A Guide to Getting Started in Missions*. Pasadena: William Carey Library, 2009.

Cross-Cultural Ministry Involvement / Short-Term Missions & Ministry Partnerships

Ernie Addicott. *Body Matters: A Guide to Partnership in Christian Mission*. Edmonds: Interdev Partnership Associates, 2005.

Chris Blumhofer and Andy Crouch. *Round Trip: A Short-Term Missions Documentary and Curriculum*. Carol Stream, IL: Christianity Today International, 2008.

Steve Corbett and Brian Fikkert. *Helping Without Hurting in Short-Term Missions*. Chicago: Moody Press, 2014.

Tim Dearborn. *Short-Term Missions Workbook: From Mission Tourists to Global Citizens*. rev. ed. Downers Grove: IVP Books, 2018.

Laurie A. Fortunak and A. Scott Moreau, eds. *Engaging the Church: Analyzing the Canvas of Short-term Missions*. Wheaton: EMIS, 2008.

Tim Gibson et al., eds. *Stepping Out: A Guide to Short Term Missions*. Seattle: YWAM Publishing, 1992.

Brian M. Howell. *Short-Term Mission: An Ethnography of Christian Travel Narrative and Experience*. Downers Grove: IVP Academic, 2012.

David A. Livermore. *Serving with Eyes Wide Open: Doing*

Short-Term Missions with Cultural Intelligence. Updated ed. Grand Rapids: Baker Books, 2013.

Ellen Livingood. *Your Focus on the World: A Step-by-Step Guide to Leading Your Whole Church into Maximum Global Impact*. Newtown: Catalyst Services, (available at http://catalystservices.org/your-focus/)

Laurie A. Occhipinti. *Making a Difference in a Globalized World: Short-term Missions that Work*. Lanham: Rowman & Littlefield, 2014.

Roger Peterson et al. *Maximum Impact Short-Term Mission*. Minneapolis: STEM Press, 2003.

Robert J. Priest, ed. *Effective Engagement in Short-Term Missions: Doing it Right!* Pasadena: William Carey Library, 2008.

Ben Laurence Ragan. *Help! We're Going on a Short-Term Trip!* 3rd ed. Marietta: CULTURELink Resources, 2011.

Daniel Rickett. *Making Your Partnership Work*. Enumclaw: WinePress Publishing, 2002.

Daniel Rickett. *Building Strategic Relationships: A Practical Guide to Partnering with Non-Western Missions*. 3rd ed. Orlando: STEM Press, 2008.

John Rowell. *Magnify Your Vision for the Small Church*. Atlanta: Northside Community Church, 1998.

J. Mack Stiles and Leeann Stiles. *Mack & Leeann's Guide to Short-Term Missions*. Downers Grove: InterVarsity Press, 2000.

David Wesley. *A Common Mission: Healthy Patterns in Congregational Mission Partnerships*. Eugene: Resource Publications, 2014.

Serving Internationals in the Community

Stephan Bauman, Matthew Soerens, and Dr. Issam Smeir.

Seeking Refuge: On the Shores of the Global Refugee Crisis. Chicago: Moody Publishers, 2016.

M. Daniel Carroll R. *Christians at the Border: Immigration, the Church, and the Bible.* 2nd ed. Grand Rapids, Brazos Press, 2013.

James K. Hoffmeier. *The Immigration Crisis: Immigrants, Aliens, and the Bible.* Wheaton: Crossway, 2009.

Matthew Kaemingk. *Christian Hospitality and Muslim Immigration in an Age of Fear.* Grand Rapids: Wm.B. Eerdmans Publishing Co., 2018.

Kathleen Leslie et al. *Church Leader's Guide to Immigration.* Baltimore: World Relief, 2014.

Tom Phillips & Bob Norsworthy. *The World at Your Door: Reaching International Students in Your Home, Church, and School.* Minneapolis: Bethany House Publishers, 1997.

Rajendra K. Pillai. *Reaching the World in Our Own Backyard.* Colorado Springs: Waterbrook Press, 2003.

Neal Pirolo. *Internationals Who Live Among Us: Doing World Missions at Home.* San Diego: Emmaus Road International, 2013.

Matthew Soerens and Jenny Yang. *Welcoming the Stranger: Justice, Compassion & Truth in the Immigration Debate.* Revised and expanded. Downers Grove: IVP Books, 2018.

Multicultural Church Ministry

David A. Anderson. *Multicultural Ministry: Finding Your Church's Unique Rhythm.* Grand Rapids: Zondervan, 2004.

Anthony B. Bradley, ed. *Aliens in a Promised Land: Why Minority Leadership is Overlooked in White Christian Churches and Institutions.* Phillipsburg: P&R Publishing, 2013.

Victor H. Cuartas. *Empowering Hispanic Leaders: An Online Model.* Virginia Beach: Mission 2819, 2009.

Mark DeYmaz. *Building a Healthy Multi-Ethnic Church: Mandates, Commitments, and Practices of a Diverse Congregation.* San Francisco: Jossey-Bass, 2007.

Mark DeYmaz and Bob Whitesel. *re:MIX: Transitioning Your Church to Living Color.* Nashville: Abingdon Press, 2016.

Mark DeYmaz and Harry Li. *Ethnic Blends: Mixing Diversity into Your Local Church.* Grand Rapids: Zondervan, 2010.

Mark DeYmaz and Harry Li. *Leading a Healthy Multi-Ethnic Church: Seven Challenges and How to Overcome Them.* Grand Rapids: Zondervan, 2010.

Ken Uyeda Fong. *Pursuing the Pearl: A Comprehensive Resource for Multi-Asian Ministry.* Valley Forge: Judson Press, 1999.

Wayne Gordon & John M. Perkins. *Do All Lives Matter?: The Issues We Can No Longer Ignore and the Solutions We All Long For.* Grand Rapids: Baker Books, 2017.

Bryan Loritts, ed. *Letters to a Birmingham Jail: A Response to the Words and Dreams of Dr. Martin Luther King, Jr.* Chicago: Moody Publishers, 2014.

Gary L. McIntosh and Alan McMahan. *Being the Church in a Multi-Ethnic Community: Why It Matters and How It Works.* Indianapolis: Wesleyan Publishing House, 2012.

Viji Nakka-Cammouf and Timothy Tseng, eds. *Asian-American Christianity: A Reader.* Castro Valley: The Institute for the Study of Asian American Christianity, 2009.

Elizabeth Conde-Frazier, S. Steve Kang, and Gary A. Parrett. *A Many Colored Kingdom: Multicultural Dynamics for Spiritual Formation.* Grand Rapids: Baker Book House, 2004.

Curtiss Paul DeYoung et al. *United by Faith: The Multiracial Congregation as an Answer to the Problem of Race.* New York: Oxford University Press, 2003.

David Ng, ed. *People on the Way: Asian North Americans*

Discovering Christ, Culture, and Community. Valley Forge: Judson Press, 1996.

Manuel Ortiz. *The Hispanic Challenge: Opportunities Confronting the Church.* Downers Grove: InterVarsity Press, 1993.

Manuel Ortiz. *One New People: Models for Developing a Multiethnic Church.* Downers Grove: InterVarsity Press, 1996.

M. Sydney Park, Soong-Chan Rah, and Al Tizon, eds. *Honoring the Generations: Learning with Asian North American Congregations.* Valley Forge: Judson Press, 2012.

John M. Perkins. *One Blood: Parting Words to the Church on Race and Love.* Chicago: Moody Publishers, 2018.

Spencer Perkins and Chris Rice. *More Than Equals: Racial Healing for the Sake of the Gospel.* rev. ed. Downers Grove: InterVarsity Press, 2000.

Soong-Chan Rah. *Many Colors: Cultural Intelligence for a Changing Church.* Chicago: Moody Publishers, 2010.

Stephen A. Rhodes. *Where Nations Meet: The Church in a Multicultural World.* Downers Grove: InterVarsity Press, 1998.

Doug Serven, ed. *Heal Us, Emmanuel: A Call for Racial Reconciliation, Representation, and Unity in the Church.* Oklahoma City: White Blackbird Books, 2016.

Paul Tokunaga. *Invitation to Lead: Guidance for Emerging Asian American Leaders.* Downers Grove: InterVarsity Press, 2003.

Randy Woodley. *Living in Color: Embracing God's Passion for Ethnic Diversity.* Downers Grove: InterVarsity Press, 2001.

George Yancey. *One Body One Spirit: Principles of Successful Multiracial Churches.* Downers Grove: InterVarsity Press, 2003.

Church Leadership & Missions

Richard R. Deridder & Roger S. Greenway. *Let the Whole*

World Know: Resources for Preaching on Missions. Grand Rapids: Baker Publishing Group, 1988.

David Horner. *When Missions Shape the Mission: You and Your Church Can Reach the World*. Nashville: B&H Publishing Group, 2011.

John R. Mott. *The Pastor and Modern Missions: A Plea for Leadership in World Evangelization*. New York: Student Volunteer Movement for Foreign Missions, 1904.

Andrew Murray. *Key to the Missionary Problem*. rep. Ft. Washington, PA: Christian Literature Crusade, 1979.

John Piper. *Brothers, We Are Not Professionals: A Plea to Pastors for Radical Ministry*, updated and expanded ed. Nashville: Broadman & Holman Publishers, 2015.

Ralph D. Winter and Steven C. Hawthorne, eds. *Perspectives on the World Christian Movement: A Reader*. 4th ed. Pasadena: William Carey Library, 2009.

Future Missionaries

Todd Ahrend. *In This Generation: Looking to the Past to Reach the Present*. Colorado Springs: Book Villages, 2010.

A.B. Bruce. *The Training of the Twelve*. rep. Grand Rapids: Kregel Publications, 1988.

Ann Dunagan. *The Mission Minded Child: Raising a New Generation to Fulfill God's Purpose*. Colorado Springs: Authentic Publishing, 2007.

Paul Borthwick. *Youth and Missions: Expanding Your Students' Worldview*. 2nd ed. Waynesboro, GA: OM Literature, 1998.

Edmund Chan. *Mentoring Paradigms: Reflections on Mentoring, Leadership and Discipleship*. Oklahoma City: Lifestyle Impact Ministries, 2008.

Victor H. Cuartas. *Empowering Hispanic Leaders: An Online Model*. Virginia Beach: Mission 2819, 2009.

Glenn Hanna. *Building Missionaries: Fostering Souls for Success on the Field.* Pittsburgh: Urban Press, 2018.

Dr. David Harley. *Preparing to Serve: Training for Cross-Cultural Mission.* Pasadena: William Carey Library, 1995.

Steve Hoke & Bill Taylor. *Global Mission Handbook: A Guide for Crosscultural Service.* rev. Downers Grove, IL: InterVarsity Press, 2009.

Gunter Krallman. *Mentoring for Mission.* Waynesboro, GA: Gabriel Publishing, 2002.

Patrick Lai. *Tentmaking: The Life and Work of Business as Missions.* Downers Grove: InterVarsity Press, 2005.

Robert E. Logan and Sherlyn Carlton. *Coaching 101: Discover the Power of Coaching.* St. Charles: Church Smart Resources, 2003.

John McVay, gen. ed. *Ask a Missionary: Time-Tested Answers from Those Who've Been There.* Colorado Springs: Authentic Publishing, 2010.

Marv Nelson. *Unleash: Empowering the Next Generation of Leaders.* Nashville: Abingdon Press, 2018.

Richard Noble. *Recruiting a New Generation of Missionaries: Doing Missions with Older Millennials in the Christian & Missionary Alliance.* 2004. (available from author)

Jim and Judy Raymo. *Millennials and Missions: A Generation Faces a Global Challenge.* Pasadena: William Carey Library, 2014.

Steve Saccone with Cheri Saccone. *Protégé: Developing Your Next Generation of Church Leaders.* Downers Grove: IVP Books, 2012.

Steve Shadrach. *The Fuel and the Flame: Ten Keys to Ignite Your College Campus for Jesus Christ.* Conway, AR: The Body Builders, 2003.

Ryan Shaw. *Spiritual Equipping for Mission: Thriving as God's Message Bearers.* Downers Grove: InterVarsity Press, 2014.

Ryan Shaw. *Waking the Giant: The Resurging Student Mission Movement*. Pasadena: William Carey Library, 2006.

M. David Sills. *The Missionary Call: Find Your Place in God's Plan for the World*. Chicago: Moody Publishers, 2008.

Student Volunteer Movement for Foreign Missions. *Student Mission Power: Report of the First International Convention of the Student Volunteer Movement for Foreign Missions*. rep. Pasadena: William Carey Library, 1979.

Joel Sutton, ed. *Whom Shall We Send? Understanding the Essentials of Sending Missionaries*. Self-Published, CreateSpace, 2016.

Paul Tokunaga. *Invitation to Lead: Guidance for Emerging Asian American Leaders*. Downers Grove: InterVarsity Press, 2003.

David L. Watson and Paul D. Watson. *Contagious Disciple Making: Leading Others on a Journey of Discovery*. Nashville: Thomas Nelson, 2014.

Mabel Williamson. *Have We No Rights? A Frank Discussion of the "Rights" of Missionaries*. Self-published, Create Space, 2010.

J. Christy Wilson, Jr. *Today's Tentmakers: Self-Support—An Alternative Model for Worldwide Witness*. Wheaton: Tyndale House Publishers, Inc., 1979.

David and Lorene Wilson, eds. *Pipeline: Engaging the Church in Missionary Mobilization*. Littleton: William Carey Press, 2018.

Marsha Woodard. *To Timbuktu & Beyond: A Guide to Getting Started in Missions*. Pasadena: William Carey Library, 2009.

David Wraight. *The Next Wave: Empowering the Generation That Will Change Our World*. Colorado Springs: Navpress, 2007.

Calling and Vocation

Andy Crouch. *Culture Making: Recovering Our Creative Calling*. Downers Grove: InterVarsity Press, 2008.

Steven Garber. *Visions of Vocation: Common Grace for the Common Good.* Downers Grove: InterVarsity Press, 2014.

Os Guinness. *The Call: Finding and Fulfilling the Central Purpose of Your Life.* Nashville: W Publishing Group, 1998.

Lee Hardy. *The Fabric of this World: Inquiries into Calling, Career Choice, and the Design of Human Work.* Grand Rapids: Wm.B. Eerdmans Publishing Co., 1990.

Skye Jethani. *Futureville: Discover Your Purpose for Today by Reimagining Tomorrow.* Nashville: Thomas Nelson, 2013.

Mark Labberton. *Called: The Crisis and Promise of Following Jesus Today.* Downers Grove: InterVarsity Press, 2014.

Amy L. Sherman. *Kingdom Calling: Vocational Stewardship for the Common Good.* Downers Grove: InterVarsity Press, 2011.

M. David Sills. *The Missionary Call: Find Your Place in God's Plan for the World.* Chicago: Moody Publishers, 2008.

James Emery White. *Serious Times: Making Your Life Matter in an Urgent Day.* Downers Grove: InterVarsity Press, 2004.

Millennials and Generation Z Insights

Chap Clark. *Hurt 2.0: Inside the World of Today's Teenagers.* Grand Rapids: Baker Academic, 2011.

Tim Elmore. *Generation iY: Our Last Chance to Save Their Future.* Atlanta: Poet Gardener Publishing, 2010.

Patricia Hersch. *A Tribe Apart: A Journey Into the Heart of American Adolescence.* New York: Fawcett Columbine, 1998.

Richard Noble. *Recruiting a New Generation of Missionaries: Doing Missions with Older Millennials in the Christian & Missionary Alliance.* 2004. (available from author)

Don Tapscott. *Growing Up Digital: The Rise of the Net Generation.* New York: McGraw-Hill, 1998.

Jean Twenge, Ph.D. *Generation Me: Why Today's Young*

Americans are More Confident, Assertive, Entitled—and More Vulnerable Than Ever Before. New York: Free Press, 2006.

Jean Twenge, Ph.D. *iGen: Why Today's Super-Connected Kids are Growing Up Less Rebellious, More Tolerant, Less Happy—and Completely Unprepared for Adulthood.* New York: Atria Books, 2017.

James Emery White. *Meet Generation Z: Understanding and Reaching the New Post-Christian World.* Grand Rapids: Baker Books, 2017.

ABOUT THE AUTHOR

Richard Noble is the founder and director of the Center for Missional Engagement in Pittsburgh, where he lives with his wife, Amy. He also serves as a pastor and missions mobilizer with The Christian & Missionary Alliance, as well as adjunct faculty at Geneva College and Crown College. He earned a BA in Speech Communication from Geneva College and a MDiv and DMin in Missions & Cross-Cultural Studies from Gordon-Conwell Theological Seminary.

www.ingramcontent.com/pod-product-compliance
Lightning Source LLC
Chambersburg PA
CBHW021141090426
42740CB00008B/879